HANDLING PUBLICITY
THE RIGHT WAY

HANDLING PUBLICITY
THE RIGHT WAY

John Venables

RIGHT WAY

Typeset in 10½ pt Times by Letterpart Ltd., Reigate, Surrey.
Printed and bound in Great Britain by Cox & Wyman Ltd., Reading, Berkshire.

The *Right Way* series is published by Elliot Right Way Books, Brighton Road, Lower Kingswood, Tadworth, Surrey, KT20 6TD, U.K.

THE AUTHOR

John Venables is a media training consultant and freelance broadcast journalist. He is a former BBC science and environment correspondent and has many years' experience as a reporter and producer in BBC local radio and regional television. He is also a journalism trainer and a Press Fellow of Wolfson College, Cambridge.

ACKNOWLEDGEMENTS

Several people helped this book through its gestation. I am very grateful to Tim Bishop, Anne Campbell, Lesley Cooke, Gerard Le Claire, Kim Riley and Alison Sargent for their advice, suggestions and useful criticism.

For Tom

CONTENTS

PREFACE

Handling publicity the right way can provide you or your organisation with the equivalent of thousands of pounds worth of
promotion – yet handling publicity is not advertising. It can
enable you to put your message across to a mass audience
efficiently and effectively – but it's not marketing. It can help
you swing public opinion in your favour – but it's not public
relations.

Handling publicity is all about using modern mass communications to your advantage, to help you market a product or
service, to educate or inform the public or to manipulate public
opinion at minimal cost to you or your company.

Knowing how to play the media game can also protect you if
things go wrong. Bad publicity can be expensive for your wallet,
your reputation or the image of your organisation. Handling the
media the right way will help you save yourself a lot of heartache
and unnecessary expense.

This book will give you the skills and the knowledge you need
to attract public attention if you want to be in the limelight – and
to cope with it if you don't. It will show you how to obtain
positive publicity, how to interest the media in your story, how to
handle a newspaper, radio or television interview effectively and
how to turn a crisis into an opportunity. What's more, it's
designed to help you save money, not spend it.

1

USING PUBLICITY TO *YOUR* ADVANTAGE

It was November 4th, and members of the Local History Society in the tiny English village of Manuden wanted to publicise their Bonfire Night party. They decided to contact the new BBC local radio station, BBC Essex, which happened to be launching its service the following day. The society secretary duly dispatched a note to the station asking for a free 'plug' on air. Almost as an afterthought she mentioned that the party would not be named for Guy Fawkes, as is customary, because the society had uncovered strong evidence that the unfortunate Mr Fawkes was innocent, framed by the trial judge who happened to be a former resident of Manuden.

Within hours, Manuden's modest celebrations became the most famous bonfire party in Britain. The tale of the unjust Justice of west Essex seized the media's interest and the secretary's house was soon besieged by reporters. The story received wide coverage on two local radio stations, two regional television news programmes, the prestigious national Radio 4 programme 'Today', a national television news programme for children and a number of local and national newspapers. Manuden Local History Society had put itself on the map *and* acquired publicity worth hundreds of thousands of pounds, all for the price of a postage stamp.

The power of publicity
The lesson the members of Manuden's Local History Society stumbled across was this: if you have a message it's no good being modest, you have to tell the world, and one of the best ways to do that is to get the media on your side. Newspaper, radio and television journalists are paid to tell people what's going on

in their communities. Play your cards right and the journalists will do the donkey work of marketing for you and it won't cost you anything. If you have the right story at the right time and you're willing to put yourself out to be interviewed you can achieve publicity which would not be possible in any other way.

Newspapers, radio and television reach a high proportion of the population. Explain your message through the mass media and you are speaking directly to thousands, even millions of people. It's like having a front door key to all the households you need to talk to. Whether you're a politician canvassing for votes, a manufacturer promoting a product, or a spokesman for a cause, if you can get your message onto the radio or television – or into the newspapers – it will reach the mass audience you're looking for.

Why should I want publicity?
You can use the media to:

- inform the public
- influence the public

The right story at the right time can attract massive media interest with next-to-no effort.

- influence other decision makers
- 'sell' a product or a concept
- educate the public
- protect or enhance your organisation's image.

Inform the public

You may want to explain why your organisation is pursuing a particular policy or action. If the public doesn't know what you're up to you could create unnecessary opposition and ill-feeling. Ignorance or misunderstanding of your activities can be dispelled by putting your arguments across convincingly and authoritatively through the media. For instance, if you run a cable TV company and you want to justify workmen digging up the pavements to lay cable ducts, then appearing on TV or local radio or in the local paper will help you explain to all those affected what you're doing and why.

Influence the public

You can use the media to determine the way people think or behave. People rely on television, radio and the newspapers to tell them about the world, the developments which may affect them and the policies and events which shape their lives. If you want to alter the way the public perceives an issue, or you want to change the way people behave, use the media to put your message across.

If, for example, you represent an environmental pressure group and you want to stop people using furniture made from irreplaceable tropical hardwoods, then your most effective soap box would be the newspaper columns and radio and television news and current affairs programmes. You will be talking directly to the consumer who buys the products, and if your argument is convincing and persuasive there's a good chance it will have an impact.

Influence other decision makers

When you appear on radio or television, or are quoted in the newspapers, what you say will be read and heard not just by the general public but also by people whose influence may be important to you. Councillors, council officers, politicians of all shades, local business leaders, even Government ministers, may be swayed by your arguments and act accordingly. If you are trying to persuade local government officials to approve a by-pass for your village, for instance, putting your arguments across forcefully and persuasively in the local media will have considerably more impact than a meeting in the village hall.

Sell a product or a concept

If you're an inventor or manufacturer, publicity may help you secure investment or attract the interest of the buying public. Too many companies and organisations are sitting on a small gold mine, potentially good stories about products or policies which never see the light of day, either because no-one realises their potential for good publicity or because of a reluctance to contact the media under any circumstances. Get your product into the news and you'll achieve valuable and influential publicity – free!

The media are wary of carrying stories which are poorly disguised advertisements, but provided there is a reasonable excuse to run a story about a product in the news journalists will usually be happy to oblige. For example, a 'new' washing powder would not qualify as news unless it is a genuine breakthrough. If the manufacturer can show that the same product is revolutionary, and will, say, wash clothes clean at room temperature, the new powder will attract widespread media interest.

The media can also be used to 'soften' the market as a prelude to an advertising campaign. The launch of Microsoft's *Windows 95* computer operating system in 1995 was marked by a huge advertising campaign which was rumoured to have cost the company tens of millions of pounds. The sheer size and expense of the campaign drew widespread media interest and in the run-up to the launch *Windows 95* became the focus of numerous newspaper articles and broadcast news items. This news coverage added immeasurably to the impact and the authority of the advertising campaign at no cost to Microsoft.

Educate the public

You can use newspapers, radio and television to improve public understanding of your subject. Science is a good example of a field where this works successfully. The gap between the frontiers of science and public understanding is widening and some educators are worried the general public is ever less aware of new discoveries. Patrick Moore and a score of other popular scientists have found the media to be a perfect vehicle with which to communicate the excitement of scientific developments to a mass audience.

Protect your organisation's image – or your own
Things go wrong and when they do the public and the media will want to know why. If you duck your head in the sand and hope the problem will go away you may make things worse. Bad publicity can cost you and your organisation money, and catastrophic loss of public confidence. Handling publicity the *wrong* way can mean lost opportunities, both in terms of money and influence over public opinion.

Never say "No comment"
If the worst happens, you can use the media to your advantage. You may think the simplest way to deal with the media in a crisis is to pull up the drawbridge, prepare for a siege and refuse to say anything. This may save you trouble in the short term. You won't have to talk to irritating reporters, issue press releases and try to remember to get up at some unearthly hour of the morning and travel miles to give a brief radio interview. However, refusing to comment will inevitably make it appear you have something to hide. We have all seen the television interviewee who rushes past the cameras, face half obscured by a raincoat, snapping "I have nothing to say" as s/he heads for the safety of the car and home. The impression left with the audience is that the person was 'guilty as charged', even though this might not in fact be the case.

Refusing to comment can lose you a valuable opportunity to put your case or point of view across to the public. Even in the darkest situation there are usually some positive factors you can pluck from the ashes; if you don't talk to the media, you are not going to be able to put across this positive information to your advantage. Media exposure, even in a crisis, can usually be turned to good account. By stressing the positive and by being clear what message you want to put over, you can diffuse tension, clear up misunderstandings and allay public fears.

Inevitably you *will* occasionally make errors, you *will* have problems, and you *will* be found out. When this happens, admit the fault and explain what action you've taken to ensure it won't happen again. With less cover up and more honesty Watergate would never have become the huge story it did. 'No White Wash at the White House' was a great headline – but a big mistake!

How can I be sure it's *my* message which gets across?
People often worry about the media's 'hidden' agenda. The fact
is, journalists will not usually seek to catch you out unless your
position is at best open to question and at worst clearly wrong-
headed or contrary to the public interest. Most media interviews
are simply intended to draw out information about a situation and
pass it on to the public. If you are still concerned the journalist is
trying to do the dirty on you there's a simple solution: have an
agenda of your own!

Never speak to the media just because you feel you have to,
or because the journalist has asked you to. It's a free society and
you're not obliged to put your neck on the block of public
opinion. The only reason for you to talk to radio, television or
newspapers is that you can see some benefit to yourself in doing
so. The media is a hugely powerful and influential communications tool which you can use to inform, influence and manipulate the public and other decision makers. Whatever the
situation, stop and think: how can I use this tool to my
advantage? With the right preparation and a knowledge of the
rules of the media game you can put forward an agenda, hidden
or otherwise, which promotes *your* interests, or those of the
organisation you represent.

The skills you need to handle the media to your advantage can
be learned, just like any other. You don't have to be a public
relations expert or a 'spin doctor' to communicate effectively. In
the chapters which follow, you will discover all the knowledge
and tips you need to interest the media in your message and put it
across effectively, to handle media interviews confidently, and
ensure that the message which goes out is the one you intended.

2

PLANNING A PUBLICITY CAMPAIGN

Let's assume that you want publicity. Running a successful publicity campaign means doing your homework. You need to work out what you want to say, to whom, how, and what you hope to achieve. It will only work if you plan the campaign thoroughly. You need to decide:

- your message
- your target audience
- the best vehicle to put your message across.

What's my message?
Decide what you want to say to the public and why you want to say it. It might be as simple as inviting your neighbours to a car boot sale. At the other extreme you may work for an organisation which is trying to push through a controversial policy change. The principle is the same: to communicate effectively with the public, you need to be clear about what it is you're trying to tell people.

Products
The first thing to realise is that you never sell a product, you persuade people to buy a benefit. Decide what the marketing people call the Unique Selling Point of your product and spell that out to the public. For example, let's suppose you have developed a new mouse trap. Clearly you want people to buy it so you need publicity (people aren't psychic and if no-one knows your product exists they won't make a bee-line for your door). So why should they buy it? People buy mouse traps to dispose of a

rodent problem; if your mouse trap works better than others then the public will be interested in it.

Does your product have subsidiary advantages, or does the benefit gained carry a cost which may outweigh its attractions? More dead mice means more bodies on the kitchen floor. If your product also works humanely then your success should be assured. People are more likely to buy a mouse trap which doesn't leave blood stains on the floor and mangled corpses which have to be explained away to gagging children!

Commerce and industry

If you're running a company there may be any number of messages you wish to get across to the public, to employees, or to other firms in your line of business.

You may want to reassure the public over the safety of production processes, or explain activities which will affect the community in some way. A policy of openness will help build a positive image of your company in the public consciousness.

You might want to explain changes in labour relations policy. If you're being forced to restructure your company, setting out the reasons for the changes and the steps you are taking to cushion the blow can help promote your company's image for responsible and caring management. It will also defuse potential confrontations with the work force.

You may need to influence or communicate with others in the same field. Putting across positive messages to competitors and support industries at crucial times can help prevent market instabilities or loss of confidence.

Politics

The essence of politics is controlled communication – with voters, with the public in general, with civil servants and with other politicians. The messages you put out – and their timing – will help you achieve your goals as a politician. Ask yourself: Whom do I want to influence? What do I want the end result to be?

Charities

Charities raise money by increasing public awareness of their particular cause, so publicity is vital if a charity is to be success- ful. To be effective, that publicity has to be carefully targeted and the message has to be right. Simply asking for money isn't enough. People don't give away money to causes they don't understand, or which don't have a relevance to them. They think first about helping themselves, then close relatives, then friends and finally members of their immediate community. Without persuasion people will see no reason to dig into their pockets to help strangers. If you can bridge the 'understanding gap' between the public and the subject of your charity then the money will start to roll in.

If your charity is humanitarian, point up similarities between communities; if the common humanity of the charity's focus group is highlighted, the public will be encouraged to treat them as members of their *own* community. Effectively, the message is: these people are starving yet they have home lives, they cook, they chat, they have children – they are like you and they need your help. This approach was applied very successfully in the Live Aid campaign to raise money for victims of war and drought in Ethiopia in the mid 1980s. The power of the media and the pop music industry was harnessed to force the public to understand and empathise with the vast scale of the humanitarian disaster.

If the charity's work involves research or an issue which isn't directly relevant to the public, and hasn't a direct human focus, the message to the public should appeal to people's self-interest. A cancer research charity won't attract public support with the news that it's doing worthy research into carcinogens. It *will* raise money if the clear message is: help us and we may be able to prevent a disease which could kill *you* or the ones *you* love.

Campaigns
Much the same principles apply if you're trying to win public support for a cause. Cynical or indifferent members of the public will ask why it matters *to them,* so your message should highlight the relevance of the issue to your target audience. If, for example, you're trying to save the Philippine rain forest, show how saving the rain forest will benefit *your* public. If you point out that saving the trees will help prevent global warming and safeguard obscure plants which may offer cures for disease, people will see a reason for contributing to your cause. If you're campaigning for a by-pass for your village your message needs to highlight the benefits of a by-pass in dramatic terms which spell out the negative implications if you don't get one.

What's my target audience?

Tailor your message to the market. Who do you want your message to reach? If it's a clearly defined group, then your job is relatively easy. You may be a scientist wanting to communicate details of a new discovery to your peers, or a local campaigner hoping to raise local support for a new by-pass. You may be an employer wanting to improve your image in the local community, or a flood prevention engineer who needs to explain forthcoming drainage works to people in the area. In each case defining your audience is simple; having done so, the next step – selecting the right *vehicle* for your message – is straightforward.

The greater challenge comes when you need to communicate to a mass audience. The 'public' is a chaotic amalgam of thousands, even millions, of different individuals, each with different needs, aspirations and opinions. How do you make your message interesting to such a vaguely defined audience?

The people alphabet

One way of deciding who you want to reach with your message is to assess who's who in the community. Advertisers – who are very careful to target their campaigns accurately – split people into groups determined by their social status and their spending power.

A	Top managers and decision makers
B	Senior managers, professionals
C1	'White collar' supervisory staff, craftsmen
C2	'Blue collar' supervisory staff, 'white collar' workers
D	Skilled manual workers
E	Unskilled manual workers

These categories are based on three factors: power, income and spending habits. According to the advertisers each group has fairly clearly defined needs, goals and aspirations which can be used to target marketing campaigns. You can use these categories too. They will help you tailor the content of your message and decide the medium you are going to use to put the message across. For instance, if you are publicising an expensive hotel there would be little point in targeting those on low incomes. If, on the other hand, you are trying to interest people in a new cut-price burger bar you will waste time and effort focusing your publicity on those who can afford an upmarket restaurant.

There are anomalies to this 'socio-economic scale'. For instance, how would you categorise someone with a so-called 'working class' background who has won the Lottery? Many pundits are trying to find a workable alternative. Some of these new models take into account attitudes and lifestyles rather than social class and income, an approach which many feel more accurately reflects the way our society is structured.

The role of women is particularly significant when targeting a message at the public. Surveys have shown that in many households the wife/mother figure is the most influential. She makes most decisions about what the family eats, where it seeks entertainment and which products it purchases.

How do I get the message across?

Match the medium to the message and your market. If you simply want to publicise a school fête, posters on village notice-boards may reach all the people you want to attract. At the other extreme you may represent a large organisation and want to target a new service, product or policy at a mass audience. In this case you will need to consider using newspapers, radio and television – even the Internet!

The poster campaign

Printing and distributing posters is an effective way of publicising small events, such as church and school fêtes, car boot sales or promoting a local campaign or cause. It costs money to print posters and takes time to stick them up, so they should only be considered a valid option for publicising events within a limited geographical area.

Make the poster eye-catching. Bright colours, especially dayglo pigments, are a must if your poster is to stand out from the competition. If you use white paper, make the design of the poster bold and attractive.

Keep your message simple. Stick to a catchy one or two word headline and then simply include details of the event; where, when and so forth. If your poster is intended to whip up public support for an issue, a few lines of explanation will be necessary to make clear what the campaign is all about. Briefly highlight why the person reading the poster should be concerned, and what s/he can do about it. Keep some detail back, if possible. The public is more likely to turn up at your meeting or event if they are intrigued to find out more or see what will happen. The British Gas privatisation poster campaign was a good example of this technique. It centred on the slogan "Tell Sid". This was an enigmatic 'teaser' intended to intrigue the public and get people talking. This then set the stage for a further two steps in the publicity campaign which progressively revealed more detail about the privatisation programme.

Having said that, few groups will have the necessary funding or the time to mount a progressive poster campaign. If you're organising a meeting, a fête or some sort of entertainment you will need to make sure that all the essential details are on the poster: *What* is happening? *When* is it happening (day and date)? *Where* is it happening? *How* people get in [i.e. 'tickets on the door', or who to contact, or 'all welcome'] and the price, if appropriate. Do make sure that someone – preferably unconnected with the event or campaign – reads through the proposed poster to check that everything that needs to be said has been included. It's surprising how easy it is to miss out something essential when you're immersed in the planning and know all the detail by heart!

Create a professional look. A shabby poster won't look 'arty', it will simply appear amateurish. Have the poster professionally printed if possible. If you have access to a home or office computer with the right software try designing your own poster using one of the many easy-to-use Desk Top Publishing (DTP) packages which are available from computer shops.

Pick the right location. Sticking up posters anywhere is a scatter gun approach which wastes resources and may also get you into trouble. Fly-posting is illegal on public or highway property, and posters should only be put up on private property if you have the owner's permission. Choose sites where people congregate, such as bus shelters, train stations and canteen notice boards.

The leaflet drop

If you want to ensure your message goes into every household in an area consider a 'flyer' or simple leaflet. These are relatively cheap and simple to produce in quantity. The leaflet drop has two drawbacks. Someone has to distribute them and that can take a lot of organising, time and effort, even if friends or relations are willing to deliver them free. The other problem is that a leaflet drop has a very low 'hit rate'. Don't think because you have distributed leaflets to five hundred homes, five hundred families will turn up to your event. The chances are that 99 in every 100 of your leaflets will end up, unread, in the waste paper bin.

If you are still keen to go ahead, make the leaflet as interesting and attractive as possible. Keep the message simple, include all relevant details (and have someone else check them!) and make your leaflet stand out by bold use of colour and professional-style printing. Pay attention to small details like spelling and grammar, particularly if you are using a leaflet to advertise a service. Its quality will determine the image the reader has of your work. A sloppily produced, dog-eared leaflet won't give potential customers confidence!

Using the Internet

Electronic publishing – putting messages onto the Internet – is likely to become an increasingly powerful publicity tool as more and more people join the Information Super Highway.

The Internet connects all computers which are linked to it, whether they are commercial mainframe computers or the back bedroom PC. Once hooked up to this network (a relatively simple process) you can send instantaneous electronic messages, called *e-mail*, around the world in seconds. You can also access special information files contained in the memory banks of computers linked to a part of the Internet called the 'World Wide Web'. These 'home sites' are electronic 'posters' which can be read by anyone with the right equipment. Once logged on to the Internet, you simply type in the address of the site you require and bingo . . . you're there, even if you are in London and the site was loaded onto a computer in Tokyo.

Many individuals and organisations have realised the publicity potential of these 'home sites' as a powerful alternative to the conventional media. Information on sports clubs, railway societies, political pressure groups and a host of other organisations is already available. Shops are setting up home sites which contain catalogues and price lists, clubs are touting for members by featuring their activities and campaigners are promoting their causes. If it's appropriate to your needs, you too should consider using the Web to put *your* message across.

Using the media

The common sense aim of anyone seeking publicity is to reach the maximum number of people as cheaply as possible. If you know how to handle the media, you can reach a very large audience at minimal cost.

The way to free publicity is to get your message into the news. In Britain there are, at the time of writing, 221 local radio stations (39 BBC and 182 commercial), 33 regional television centres (18 BBC and 15 independent companies), five national BBC radio channels and five national TV networks, as well as a plethora of satellite and cable channels. Nearly all broadcast news or current affairs programmes and every week hundreds of hours of airtime need to be filled. There are dozens of local newspapers, as well as the national newspapers, each with scores of pages which have to be filled with stories. More than ever before the media are looking for events and issues to cover . . . and yours could be one of them.

The print media

Newspapers, magazines and trade journals are a powerful and influential means of reaching the public.

Local papers exist to serve a specific urban area, like a city or large town, or sometimes a large rural district with a number of small communities. Local papers are sometimes published daily, others come out weekly. They focus on issues and events which affect the local community. To attract maximum publicity you need to relate your story to people and concentrate on the 'human angle'. If it's an education related issue – for example, you are campaigning for smaller class sizes – find a child who failed to learn to read because s/he 'slipped through the net'. If you've formed a community-help group, highlight the plight of an elderly lady who hasn't been able to mow her lawn or take her rubbish out for weeks. The local papers will lap it up!

Local papers of the traditional kind cost money, so their distribution is limited by the number of people who are willing to pay for their local information. That in turn will limit the number of people you can reach with your story. This isn't a problem with the so-called *'free sheets'*. These are distributed free of charge and go through every door in the district. They are therefore an excellent source of publicity as they reach the maximum number of local readers. The 'frees' also employ very few news staff, so they are often desperate for good stories and information to fill their pages. You should have little trouble getting your story into the local free paper no matter how mundane the subject.

Regional papers serve a wider population. If your message is relevant to people living in a particular region which matches the distribution area of a regional paper, you will save yourself the effort of contacting a number of local papers.

National newspapers are clearly an attractive option if you want to put your message across to the widest possible readership. However, the nationals differ from their regional and local cousins in several significant ways and you need to know what those differences are if you are to use the national newspapers to your advantage.

- The nationals serve a country-wide audience with a diet of news which will interest the community as a whole. This means they will only be interested in events, issues or personalities which will have a relevance to people throughout the country. While everyone's national news is someone's local story, your message will only get into the national papers if it is sufficiently odd, quirky, or important to interest a broader public.

- National papers usually have a political bias or represent the views of a particular section of the national population. In Britain, the *Telegraph* and the *Mail* are regarded as broadly right wing in the news they publish and the way they approach or interpret issues and stories. The *Mirror* and the *Guardian* reflect the views of those whose politics are left of centre. All these papers will cover much the same stories, but the way they interpret the stories will be different. So if your story reflects on Government policy in some way you can expect to see widely differing slants in the way it is written up.

- National papers cater for different groups in the community. The choice of stories and the way they are written is carefully tailored to the needs and interests of different readerships. In Britain, there are the *broadsheets* (so called because of the size paper they are printed on) which are upmarket, and the *tabloids*, which are downmarket. The *Times* and *Telegraph* are targeted at those in socio-economic groups A and B;

tabloids such as the *Mail* and *Express* target the C1s and C2s; the *Sun* and *Mirror* reflect (some would say create) the views of those in groups D and E.

The broadsheets will be interested in a wide range of subjects, from the worthy and important to the light and quirky. The tabloids are primarily interested in strong human interest stories, preferably with an element of controversy, tragedy or sex! The tabloids will also feature the very quirky story which will catch public interest.

If your message is likely to be of interest to a specialist audience then magazines and the trade, professional and specialist press could be the vehicle you need. Look along any newsagent's shelves and you will see that in Britain alone there are hundreds of titles covering every subject under the sun, from aquaria to zoology. Some take a popular approach and sell to a large readership. *Good Housekeeping* for instance has a circulation of over half a million and each issue is read by more than two and a half million readers. Others are learned journals with a small specialist readership. Ignore the potential of magazines and the specialist press and you could be missing out on an important and useful source of publicity. Your local library will have a copy of *Willings Press Guide* which lists every single publication in the UK, along with contact telephone numbers and addresses.

Many newspapers and the broadcast media get a proportion of their stories from *news agencies* such as the Press Association. These organisations concentrate their resources on news gathering and sell the results on to the media. Some work locally, while others operate nationally or even internationally. News agencies are often overlooked by those seeking publicity for their stories, which is a pity because they can circulate stories to a wide range of outlets with minimum effort. A story sent out to a news agency tends to snowball and gather momentum, jumping from one media outlet to another.

The broadcast media

Used properly, television and radio offer a phenomenally powerful means of communication. If you can put your message across persuasively and effectively in a radio or TV interview you will reach and influence a lot of people. Yet, perhaps because exposure on the broadcast media requires a performance on the part of the interviewee, many people and organisations have taken a long time to embrace their potential as a source of effective and free publicity. Industry in particular has tended to keep the broadcasters at arm's length. Those with a good story to tell will often ring the local newspaper but ignore the local radio or regional television station. By doing so they're missing out on a great opportunity to pass their message to the public.

The broadcast media fall into seven groups:

- community radio
- local (or regional) radio
- local television
- regional television
- national radio
- national television
- satellite television.

Community radio stations offer excellent publicity opportunities if you want your message to reach a limited area. Their target audience is very local and specialised; some stations target one community, others target a specific interest group which may be ethnic or perhaps defined by a special interest, such as one particular genre of music. If you want to practise your media skills or your message is appropriate to a community audience then contact your community radio station.

Local radio in Britain comes in two flavours: BBC and commercial. Both have a larger target audience than community radio and focus on a city, group of neighbouring towns, or a county. BBC local radio tends to appeal to an older audience largely composed of the C1, C2, D and E socio-economic groups. Independent stations target a younger audience in the same categories. (The so-called As and Bs tend to listen to network radio.) Individual local radio stations reach tens, even hundreds of thousands of listeners every day and together they command a mass audience of millions, larger than that of the national radio stations.

Commercial stations predominantly play music, though they usually have a locally based newsroom and broadcast hourly news bulletins. BBC local radio programmes are more speech-based and therefore have a voracious appetite for stories. As well as news and discussion programmes many stations also have regular 'What's on' slots – the electronic equivalent of postcards in a shop window – which can be an excellent (and free) source of grass roots publicity.

Some areas now have *local television*, especially in the big cities. Stations such as the cable TV service *'Channel One'* in London will increasingly offer a means of reaching a local audience very effectively.

Regional television, both BBC and commercial, is another source of good publicity which is often ignored by those who could use its power to reach a wide audience to their own benefit. As the name implies, each regional TV station covers a large geographical area, but the news and programmes transmitted are still local. Both commercial and BBC TV stations broadcast a number of bulletins throughout the day as well as a half hour programme in the evening and, like local radio, are hungry for news. If your story is visual and would be of interest to a regional audience your regional TV station may well be interested in covering it.

Network radio and *television* are the most influential of all the broadcast media. If your story finds its way on to the national news you can be sure it will have a massive impact. Your message will be beamed into literally millions of homes. Because everyone wants a slice of that sort of publicity the network channels are very choosy about the stories they cover, but if your tale is important, quirky or has relevance to a wide audience, national coverage may follow.

In Britain there are currently five national BBC radio channels:

- Radio 1 is a music channel, with some news, serving a young audience. It offers little potential for publicity except that closely associated with its style and audience.
- Radio 2 plays popular music and features to suit a rather older audience, and may feature issues related to the interests of its audience.
- Radio 3 is a classical music channel which offers little publicity potential unless the story is associated with the arts and serious music.
- Radio 4 is speech based with an emphasis on news and current affairs, and offers excellent publicity potential. A wide range of programmes covers everything from general news and current affairs to specialist subjects such as science and wildlife.

- Radio 5 is also news and current affairs based but with a more laid back appeal, and also offers excellent publicity potential. Radio 5 features 24 hour news and therefore has a huge appetite for stories. The channel has strong links with BBC local radio to help serve its requirements.

There are also a growing number of national commercial stations serving specific markets. For instance, Classic FM specialises in popular classic music. Other national independent stations such as Talk Radio UK look for provocative discussion areas – it's worth listening round the dial to see if one of these stations serves your purpose.

The independent stations take their news from Independent Radio News (IRN), which runs a central newsdesk in London and provides a national news service for all commercial radio outlets, including local radio stations.

National television in Britain currently has five channels: BBC 1 and 2, ITV and Channels 4 and 5. Between them these channels provide a mass audience with a wide range of programmes on every possible subject. If your story is aired on the BBC's prestigious '6 o'clock' or '9 o'clock News' or on the commercial news provider ITN's flagship 'News at 10' you will have publicity money can't buy, both in terms of the size of the audience and the authority the medium will confer on your tale. Of course, the potential for bad publicity to make its mark at this level is also that much greater. Either way, people will definitely know you are there!

The BBC offers a 24 hour television news channel as part of its expansion into digital broadcasting. This service takes its information from a wide range of BBC sources: international, national and regional. With so much airtime to fill 24 Hour News is hungry for stories and therefore offers extremely good opportunities for those seeking publicity.

Satellite television channels such as those owned by BSkyB have a large and rapidly growing following. They broadcast a range of specialist programmes and news to a national audience and therefore could be just the vehicle you need for your message. Sport, in particular, is well served, so if you're trying to publicise a minority activity it's worth knowing that the satellite channels offer publicity opportunities which simply aren't available through the more traditional television outlets. The satellite channel audience may not be as large as that currently served by the terrestrial television stations, but if you get your message onto the space waves you will still be reaching a large number of people.

By this stage in planning your publicity campaign you should have a clear idea of what your message is, who you want to send it to and the means by which you want to put it across. If you've decided to target the media, you are on the threshold of a great opportunity for creating powerful publicity. But – and there's always a but – first you have to get the media interested in your message. So what are they looking for?

3

WHAT INTERESTS THE MEDIA?

If you're going to interest the media in your story you need to understand what makes journalists 'tick'. You also need to know what they look for in a story and why.

Who are journalists?

Most journalists would say they chose their career because they were curious about the world, wanted to write for a living, or perhaps had a burning desire to put the world to rights. Many start in newspapers, usually at a local level, and stay there throughout their careers. Some move from newspapers into broadcast journalism, while others by-pass newspapers and go straight into radio or television. Most start their chosen career with a university degree of some sort, often in the humanities, history or politics, although an increasing number will have read media studies at college. Relatively few have a science or engineering background.

Many journalists work as general 'hacks', covering a huge and diverse range of subjects. It's not unknown for a local reporter to cover a story about a hedgehog hospital in the morning and interview the Prime Minister in the afternoon! General reporters are therefore unlikely to have specialist knowledge of any one field – they are the quintessential 'Jacks (or Jills) of all trades and masters of none'. Some senior journalists do specialise in particular subjects and become a correspondent covering crime, community affairs, science, environment, local government or transport stories. Because specialist reporters have the luxury of concentrating on one topic they should be better informed on your subject.

The general reporter is unlikely to have a technical education, so if yours is a technical or scientific field you should be prepared to spend a little time explaining the background to the story at a simple level if you want the reporter to get the facts right. The more the reporter understands about your story, the better s/he can communicate it.

What are journalists looking for?

Journalists trade in news. They look for stories which they think will interest their readers, listeners or viewers. Newspapers depend on large readerships to make money, both through high street sales and through advertising. The same is true of independent radio and television. Even the BBC – funded by the television licence fee – is sensitive to low audience ratings. To sell newspapers, or persuade an audience to watch a television programme or listen to the radio, news has to be something more than just information – it has to have *news value*.

What is news?

For a story to interest an audience it needs two things.

First, it has to involve *change*. Unless something has altered, then there's no story. You can't imagine a newspaper headline screaming "No change at local factory". The bigger the change the more the audience will be interested, because it may affect their lives in some way. "Factory threatens to shed five hundred local jobs" implies a big change which will affect many local people and their families.

To interest an audience the story also has to have some relevance to people's *security* – their jobs, their children's schooling or their physical safety. People wouldn't buy a newspaper to read about a small change in Government regulations which isn't going to affect anyone. On the other hand, a major outbreak of food poisoning will affect many in the community both directly and indirectly. People will want to know whether they or their families or their friends are at risk, so they'll listen to the radio, watch TV or buy newspapers to find out the extent of the threat and what's being done about it.

"Journalists always twist the facts"
Contrary to popular myth, most stories are actually published without much distortion and with no 'hidden agenda'. But journalists will always look for ways to make a story attractive to the

audience so it's important you know how this may affect the way the story is interpreted.

When a journalist is writing up your story, s/he will instinctively look for the 'angle' which will interest the public, seeking out the elements of change and pointing up their relevance to the audience. This may mean the journalist's view of the newsworthy aspects of your story is different from yours. For example, you may think that your plans to mechanise the entire production process in your factory is technically fascinating; the journalist is more likely to highlight the human angle and focus on the potential impact of your scheme on jobs. The reason is simple: new machines aren't media consumers – people are!

If you want to establish what the journalist's 'agenda' will be when s/he comes to cover your story, ask yourself two questions:

- does what I'm doing involve change, and if so, how radical is that change?
- how will that change affect people and their lives?

The answers to these two questions will give you a good indication of the news value the journalist will put on the story and the aspects of the story s/he will highlight in the report.

The skate boarding duck

Many stories are published which have no obvious implications for people's security. These often humorous or quirky tales feature as 'news in brief' (or NIB) items in newspapers and the so-called 'And finally . . .' at the end of radio or television news bulletins. Some years ago, a skate boarding duck shot to national prominence. This type of story makes news because the quirky element in the tale involves change – a deviation from the norm.

Audience research shows that radio and television audiences remember this sort of story even when they've completely forgotten more serious news items. As a result the media has an insatiable appetite for quirky stories with a strong human, or animal, content. If *your* story is that little bit off-beat, or you can highlight an aspect of the story which is different, it will attract the attention of the journalist because it will intrigue the audience.

An off-beat story will often attract a journalist's interest.

Assessing the newsworthiness of specialist stories

The first thing to accept is that, on its own, technical innovation won't interest the general public. A specialist story has to have relevance to people's daily lives. For example, details of a new type of drilling rig may well fascinate workers in the oil or gas industry but the story won't interest a general audience unless the new rig promises cheaper oil or gas, or if it means more local jobs.

It's possible to draw up a league table of the sciences and the newsworthiness of the stories they generate. The central question you have to ask is this: what obvious relevance does the science have to people? On this basis, *medical* stories top the league. Medical research affects people's health so people will always be interested in new developments. The *life sciences* in general, like psychology, get a good audience because we are interested in the way our bodies and minds work. Stories about animals also do well because we have a deep underlying interest in them. David Attenborough's television series 'Life on Earth' is regarded by many as one of the BBC's finest programmes of all time. With masterful technical skill it showed us details of the natural world we had never seen and so helped to put our own existence into context. At the other end of the scale, *chemistry* and *pure mathematics* won't interest the public unless the research has obvious and practical implications for people's lives.

If you are trying to publicise a specialist story, focus on the applications and practical implications of your product or invention. This will grab the attention of the journalist and the audience. If you wish you can *then* educate them by slipping the science in by the back door. For instance, the development of a new plastic polymer will not excite the public *per se*; if you point out this could mean cheap, thin TV screens people can hang on the wall you'll be well on the way to extensive publicity.

Practical difficulties and ... timing

Logistical problems play a major part in deciding what makes the news. Limitations such as whether the station can spare staff to cover the story or whether a journalist can physically get to the event will play a part in the editorial decision making process. Perhaps the most important of these practical considerations is *timing*.

All reporters face deadlines – the time after which production of the paper or a radio or television programme is physically impossible. Radio and television reporters, and press photographers, need time to take and process pictures or tape recorded material; newspaper reporters need to write their copy. If your event occurs too close to the journalist's deadline it may be dropped because the story can't be processed in time.

Journalists want stories which will interest their readers, viewers or listeners, and which can be covered in reasonable time and with available resources. As we have already seen, if a story is to interest the audience it should involve change, which in turn should have a real impact on the audience. If the story doesn't have an *obvious* element of change which will affect people, the journalist will seek out and highlight any such element within the story. What we will look at now is how knowing this enables you to attract the journalists' interest and ensure that *your* story gets the publicity it deserves.

4

HOW TO ATTRACT MEDIA ATTENTION

Journalists don't have a crystal ball. Unless you tell them about your story they won't know it exists. The trouble is, newsrooms are inundated with requests for publicity from companies, local authorities and interest groups all scrabbling for their place in the sun. How do you make sure it's *your* story which catches the journalists' attention?

The most common types of bait to use if you want to hook yourself a journalist are:

- the press release
- the electronic news release
- the press conference
- the media briefing.

The press release
The press release is the most common way of alerting the media to a potential story. It's a one page summary of the essential facts, packaged in such a way that it attracts the attention of a busy journalist.

If it works, you'll see your story in print or you'll get a phone call asking for more details and perhaps an interview. If so, you'll be on your way to achieving the publicity you seek. If the press release doesn't work you'll hear no more.

The essential criteria for a successful press release are that it should be distinctive, easy to read, and easy to understand.

What do I want to say?
There'll be lots you could say about your event but the function

of the press release is to attract the journalist's interest, nothing more. You therefore need to include only the bare bones of the story. The effective press release needs to supply the following essential detail only:

What	*is happening?*
Who	*is involved (or will it affect, or benefit)?*
Why	*is it happening?*
How	*will it happen?*
Where	*will it happen?*
When	*is it happening?*

Sit down with a sheet of paper or notebook and write two or three sentences against each heading. Your finished press release should be no longer than six paragraphs long.

You will probably need several attempts at this condensation process. If the event you are publicising is very complicated or has been months in preparation it can be very difficult to summarise the essential details. Be ruthless. If necessary prepare several drafts, each time seeking to achieve that crisp, simple one page outline of the event. Try each one out on a friend or colleague – or better still someone's twelve year old child. If any of them scratch their head after a quick scan of your draft, go back and try to make it even simpler.

Once you're happy that you've condensed the essential details of your story into a few brief paragraphs you need to sort them into some sort of order. The most newsworthy paragraphs should go at the top. Usually these are the *what*, and the *why* of the story. You can then arrange the other facts in order: *who*, *how*, *where*, and *when*.

Let's see how this works in practice. Let's say you're writing a press release to publicise residents' plans to block a road in a row over a village by-pass. In this case, you might decide it was the *who* and the *what* which are the most important facts to spell out first:

"Hundreds of residents in the village of Oxbury are to block a main through road next Wednesday night."

You might then want to explain *why* the demonstration is taking place:

"They're worried that heavy traffic using the busy A260

endangers children's lives after two toddlers were killed at a pelican crossing in the centre of the village.''

You could then go on to describe *how* the event will take place, or *how* the protesters hope the action will influence the situation:

''The residents want the local council to bring forward plans for a by-pass which have been repeatedly shelved for ten years.''

Having put the 'meat' of your case in the first couple of paragraphs, you can then tell the journalist *where* and *when* the event will take place. Be clear in your directions and don't assume the journalist will know what you're talking about. If you say ''outside the chairman's house'' this will mean nothing to someone from out of town. Give full directions to your event, and a clear indication of the time and date it will occur.

Keep it simple

When writing your press release don't be tempted to use technical jargon or complicated ideas. Busy journalists will not have the time to trudge through your press release, dictionary in hand. They will simply ditch it if they can't understand it easily. It will serve your purposes much better if what you write is couched in simple everyday terms. Imagine you are writing to a child or to an elderly relative. This will help you keep your message straightforward and easy to understand. For more on avoiding jargon see Chapter 7 'How to Handle a Broadcast Interview'.

Keep it short

A press release should be no longer than one, or at most two, sides of A4. Anything more will be too much for the journalist to absorb in one quick read. If your story is binned because it is long, complicated and involved you'll have wasted a lot of effort. At this stage you're simply trying to get the journalist interested in the essence of your story, so keep it short. There'll be plenty of opportunity to add further detail when the journalist phones you to find out more.

The importance of the headline

To guarantee your press release stands out, give it a clear, punchy title which tantalises and encourages the journalist to read on. No-one expects you to have the skills of the tabloid headline writer but anyone can think up two or three words which summarise the excitement of the story. Keep it short, make it snappy – and don't be afraid of a little hyperbole.

For instance, if you're launching a campaign to press for a much needed by-pass for your village "Villagers' Death Threat Warning!" is more eye catching than "Villagers call for by-pass". If you're opening a new factory, "New plant creates 100 jobs!" will have more impact than "Acme Engineering expands trading activities".

How should I produce my press release?
Make it easy for the journalist to read. Your press release should be typewritten, either on a word processor or typewriter. Hand written press releases are to be avoided. If your writing is poor the busy journalist won't have time to struggle through your hieroglyphics and your release will end up in the bin.

If you do have access to a word processor, make the most of it. At this stage you are trying to make your press release stand out. Presentation is everything and first impressions count. Modern ink jet and laser printers produce a very high quality print. They're also extensively used by large companies. A word processed press release will convey that extra element of professionalism.

Use a letterhead. Not only will it look better but your letterhead will hopefully have the essential details of address and phone, fax and e-mail numbers which the journalist can use to contact you.

Only type on one side of each sheet of paper. You might feel the inclination to save a little money by using both sides but don't be surprised if your press release gets lost or ignored. By long standing tradition journalists type on one side of a sheet of paper only – there's less danger of something important being overlooked.

Use double line spacing. The eye scans a double spaced page easily, while tightly packed single spaced writing is likely to frustrate the journalist. Double spacing is easy to achieve on a typewriter by flicking a lever. If you're using a word processor application changing the line spacing is almost as easy. Just click the appropriate tool bar button; or change the setting under 'Paragraph' on the 'Format' menu.

An advantage of using a word processor to produce your press release is that a good system will let you alter the size and the boldness of the print font. You can use this facility to make your press release more eye catching. By changing the size of the font you can make the headline stand out:

Villagers' Death Threat Warning!

[20 point Impact]

is more effective than:

Villagers' Death Threat Warning!

[12 point Arial].

Most modern word processor programmes allow you to change the font quite easily. You can either use a pull down menu or click the appropriate box in the tool bar at the top of the screen.

If you're using a typewriter you won't be able to change fonts. Instead *underline* the headline and use capital letters to make it stand out:

VILLAGERS' DEATH THREAT WARNING!

How can I provide additional information?

I've stressed the need to keep things short and simple when you're compiling the press release itself. However, there is a way you can provide more information without losing the attention of the journalist and that is to supply a separate fact sheet along with the press release. This sheet is traditionally entitled 'Notes to the Editor', though there's no reason why you should call it that. 'Further details' would suffice. The purpose of the 'Notes to the Editor' is to provide relevant material which may be useful to the journalist when s/he is writing up the story. This sheet may be typed *single space* and you don't need to be so careful about being simple and concise. In our example of the by-pass row we could include statistical details about the accidents in the village, the efforts the villagers have made to monitor traffic density, the history of their campaign for a by-pass and so on. A comprehensive 'Notes to the Editor' sheet can be very valuable to the journalist, *once* he or she is already interested in the story!

Embargoes

You may not want your story to be publicised before a certain date and time. Perhaps it involves a shareholders' meeting, or a company restructuring, and prior publicity could be awkward or even damaging. If there are good reasons why your story should not receive early publicity then feel free to impose an *embargo*. This means you don't want your story publicised until a date and time which is convenient to you.

To impose an embargo, simply write **"Embargoed until** [whatever the date and time of the embargo is]" prominently across the top of the press release.

When establishing the date and time of the embargo do bear in mind the operational requirements of the media. Many radio stations have flagship programmes which run at breakfast time. If you embargo your story until 9.30 am – half an hour after most breakfast shows go off air – you may have missed out on a valuable and influential opportunity for publicity. Many professional publicity and press officers embargo stories until midnight before the day of publication or transmission. It might seem a strange time but it's the hour *least* likely to clash with the programming and publication requirements of the media and *most* likely to offer you maximum publicity opportunities the next day.

Your embargo sets the date and time of publication or transmission, not the moment when you need to start talking to journalists. Television, radio and newspaper coverage has to be pre-planned and interviews need to be recorded and processed, often the day before. Provided journalists promise to honour the embargo be flexible about their need to prepare material in advance.

Be aware that the embargo system isn't fool-proof. In imposing an embargo you are simply requesting the media not to publish early; you have no real come-back if they do. There are two circumstances when journalists may be tempted to break an embargo. The first is if they can't see the relevance of the restriction, so don't simply embargo the story because you think it makes the press release look more 'official'. Secondly, if yours is a really strong story one medium may break the embargo to steal a march on its rivals. If this happens everyone else is likely to jump on the bandwagon and your embargo will become unworkable.

Establishing a point of contact

At the bottom of the press release be sure to include a name and phone number for more information. Make sure that person is willing to give more information and is there to give it when the journalist calls. All too frequently journalists follow up an interesting press release only to be told the person whose contact name has been given has gone on holiday for two weeks! By the time the contact has returned the journalist may well have lost interest in the story.

Make someone available for interview

If it's a relatively simple story and all the detail they need has been included newspaper journalists will often work from the press release alone. They may not even consult you, so the first indication you have that your press release has worked is when you see your story in print!

However, sound and pictures are the bread and butter of radio and television so no matter how comprehensive your press release it's very likely that the broadcast media will want to interview someone from your organisation to explain what the story is about and to give more detail. Make sure someone *is* available for interview. Again, you'd be surprised how often a journalist follows up an interesting press release, only to be told the person who can speak on the subject is away or unavailable.

If your story involves interesting sounds or visual effects broadcast journalists will want to record them. Offer interesting filming or recording possibilities in your press release.

Where should I send the press release?

Target your market. Many public relations companies send out publicity material on a blanket basis. This is a waste of money and will make you look unprofessional. Sending a photograph of a new product to a radio station (not uncommon!) is pointless and a waste of resources and money.

Think who you want to reach with your publicity. Is it other members of your trade or profession? In which case send a press release to your trade magazine. Is the story likely to interest the general public? If so, where? If you only want to reach local people, send a press release to the local paper and the local radio station. If you want to interest a regional or even national audience, target the national media and /or regional TV and radio stations.

Bear in mind the news value or quirkiness of the story has to be that much stronger to attract national coverage, but don't be faint hearted and assume your press release won't be of interest. Be bold and send a copy to every *relevant* news outlet. The most you will waste is the price of a stamp . . . and you never know, yours might be just the story the newsdesk has been waiting for.

Who should I address it to?

Once you've decided which news outlet or programme to go for it's worth taking a little time and trouble to find out *who* to send the press release to. Address your press release to them by name. If it's a story of general news interest send the press release to the News Editor. This will make sure it reaches the news planning desk (though not the News Editor, just as you are unlikely to reach the Manager when you send a letter to your bank). If yours is a specialist story and you know the station or paper you're targeting has a specialist reporter or correspondent, then send the press release to that person (e.g.: 'The Sports Editor', or 'The Environment Correspondent'), and again, if you can, use the person's name.

How should I send the press release?

The usual way to send out press releases is by fax or the conventional post. Computerised electronic 'e-mail' is certainly an option but many newsrooms are not yet geared up to receive e-mail reliably so there's always the chance your important missive may get lost in cyberspace. If you live or work nearby you can always drop your press release in by hand. If you do this, don't expect to be able to chat your project through in detail with a journalist at the time. Leave your press release at reception and wait for a phone call later, when the newsroom system has had time to digest its contents.

When should I send the press release?
Send your press releases off in good time, well before the date of
the event you are publicising. Although the media are flexible
enough to react quickly to a story if they need to, coverage of
most stories is usually pre-planned. News editors need to work
out in advance which stories they want to cover and camera
crews need to be booked and reporters allocated.

If you send in a press release a day before the event you're
publicising, or worse, on the day itself, there is a strong likelihood your story won't be covered because reporting resources
have already been allocated elsewhere. There is a chance you
may get coverage, particularly if your story is very topical or the
newsdesk diary is empty, but don't risk it. Send in your press
release at least ten days before so it can be absorbed into the
newsroom system.

How do I make sure it gets used?
You can't force the journalist to use your story, but if it's
interesting and you've submitted a well crafted press release the
chances are it will be considered.

The newsdesk is unlikely to telephone you straight away. Your
press release will be filed with others for consideration nearer the
date you've given on the press release. Though they like to have
details of an event ahead of time, journalists decide which stories
to cover just a day or two – perhaps only hours – before the
event. This is because other, bigger stories may come along and
other potential items may have to be dropped.

If you haven't heard anything a couple of days before the event
phone the newsdesk or the production office concerned and
politely ask if they are considering your story. They may say they
still haven't made up their minds, or they may say your press
release wasn't of interest. On the other hand, your phone call may
act as a memory jogger and they may welcome the opportunity to
discuss details there and then.

If your story has been abandoned don't get cross. The decision
to drop it may have been made on reasonable grounds – it clashes
with a bigger event or it's not the right material for the programme or newspaper you've approached. Having said that,
there's no harm in trying to change the journalist's mind. Sometimes a casual mention that the opposition is covering the story
can have startling effects! But if cajoling doesn't work, beefing

about exclusion will only put the journalist's back up. Accept defeat and hope for better luck next time.

Electronic news releases

The Video News Release (VNR) and the Audio News Release (ANR) are hi-tech versions of the conventional press release. These are intended to attract interest from the broadcast media by offering the story in a form the radio and television station can use at no cost or effort to the station itself. Both are 'cuckoos' in that they're intended to disguise the promoter's agenda in a form which the host station will accept. Just like a 'real' radio or television news item, the Video or Audio News Release will include interviews, sound and visual effects, and will be produced to a format which will fit the output of the majority of stations.

Both VNRs and ANRs are regarded ambivalently by news and programme editors. If the subject is non-controversial and the package well produced some stations will run them unedited; after all, it's free broadcasting. However, because VNRs and ANRs are editorially 'tainted' and biased towards their subject the BBC's policy has always been to err on the side of doubt and not use electronic news releases; many commercial stations adopt a similar cautious stance. There are exceptions, particularly if the material would be costly or difficult to acquire in any other way. Video material of military exercises and new weapons systems produced by the armed forces' own film crews is frequently used by TV outlets, as is footage of fires and other dramas shot by the emergency services.

Think twice before commissioning an electronic news release. A cheap and shoddy product will achieve nothing, whereas a quality package will cost you a good deal of money and there's no guarantee radio and television stations will use the end result. Concentrate on persuading the broadcast media to cover your story with their own resources and you may well achieve just as much positive publicity at no cost to you or your organisation.

Press conferences

The first word of advice is, except in a crisis (see Chapter 11), don't hold press conferences – they're a waste of your valuable resources. Gone are the days when you could cram dozens of journalists in a room, talk to them for half an hour, answer a few questions, issue a press pack and then open the bar, confident that your message would soon be winging its way onto the front pages of the nation's newspapers.

Press conferences don't work like that any longer. Newspaper journalists are often office bound and unlikely to turn up. Even if they do they may be out numbered by their colleagues from radio and television, and broadcasters have different demands from print journalists. Each radio and television reporter will want an exclusive interview. The individual broadcast journalist and his or her editor will want to see or hear you talking to *them* and them alone, and they won't be interested in writing up your speech because they will want to record you saying the same thing, briefly and concisely, in an interview. Take all this in the round and you will appreciate that press conferences are ineffectual in their traditional form. Your speech will be wasted on a bored, restless audience and afterwards you'll be besieged by a chaotic mêlée of journalists each clamouring for a two or three minute interview.

If you really *must* organise a press conference here are some basic guidelines.

- Don't call a press conference except on a major issue which you are sure will interest the media. News editors are reluctant to send journalists to report on a minor story which could be covered more cheaply and easily with a quick telephone interview.
- When selecting a date and time for the conference try to fit in with reporter's deadlines, and don't pick a day which you can reasonably expect will coincide with a more important event elsewhere. You obviously can't predict the train crash or other major news story which will suddenly divert the media's attention but some events, like elections, are easily avoided. Try to hold your press conference towards the beginning of the week. Most influential flagship programmes go out on weekdays only and many local and regional radio and TV stations run a restricted news service at weekends, so holding a conference on Friday will mean if it is reported in full it won't be until the following week. Many newsrooms struggle to find stories just after the weekend, so a Monday or Tuesday conference is more likely to attract a desperate producer or news editor's attention. The best *time* slot is just

before lunch. This will give reporters a chance to travel to the
conference and get back to process their reports or recordings
for early evening programmes and bulletins. If your story is
big enough, holding a press conference at noon on a Monday
could mean publicity in all the major evening bulletins and
the following day's morning papers. The same story put out at
four o'clock on Friday afternoon may not get any coverage at
all.

- Offer broadcast journalists the chance to carry out their
  interviews before the conference itself on the strict understanding that they don't publish anything until the conference
  has begun. You will avoid the media scrum which would
  otherwise ensue after the conference.

- Have a suitable backdrop on hand for television interviews and
  the press photographers. Your logo or slogan, or some other
  relevant visual aid such as a model of a project will re-enforce
  the messages you are presenting in the interview itself.

- Issue each journalist with a press release summing up the
  purpose of the conference and giving quotable quotes. Copies
  of any speeches will be useful to press reporters, but not
  broadcast journalists – they'll want to interview you instead.
  Fax copies of speeches to press journalists who haven't
  shown up. If relevant, provide press quality photographs for
  use by newspapers.

- Do provide some sort of food and drink as reporters may have
  missed their breakfast or lunch to get to the conference. They
  won't have time for a full sit down meal so a buffet is quite
  adequate. Don't go overboard laying on alcoholic drink. The
  'drunken hack' is nowadays a creature of popular myth – at
  least on duty!

- If you can afford it, provide several telephones and fax
  machines. With the rise in the number of journalists using
  laptops and modems a number of phone points to plug these
  into would be useful as well.

- Provide a 'quiet room' for one-to-one radio interviews. This
  should have basic soft furnishings such as curtains and carpet
  to improve the ambient sound quality.

The media briefing/facility visits

A better alternative to the press conference is to focus your
attentions on a small group of journalists who you know will be

interested in your subject and will give you the publicity you need. Invite them to lunch or even breakfast and spell out your message informally. Not only will the proceedings be more interactive, you can give each journalist more of your time and you won't be rushed off your feet. If a media briefing is to be successful you will have to do your homework. Invite senior reporters or specialist correspondents from different branches of the media who you think will have the clout and the experience to push your story up the news 'running order'.

Facility visits are a variation on the media briefing which allow the journalist to see, and if possible experience, the subject of the story. If you are opening an adult adventure centre you are much more likely to interest the media if you offer the journalists a trial drive in a tank than if you coop them up in your office. Every journalist loves a 'freebee', especially if it involves the travel industry; but do be wary of over-extending yourself. A now defunct airline once took a number of provincial journalists, including myself, on a first class all expenses paid trip to New York for the weekend. It was a wonderful break but I doubt if the resulting coverage generated more than a handful of potential passengers.

Be aware of the requirements of the journalists and camera crews when planning a facility visit and be flexible if they want something specific. If you're showing journalists round the flagship of your ferry line they won't be content with some general views of the ship from the shore. A good camera operator or photographer will want creative shots in the engine room or the bridge, so be prepared to open doors which are normally closed. Make clear in advance what camera/filming/recording opportunities will be available. Also, don't make the timetable for the visit too tight. TV camera operators need time to get the sort of creative shots necessary for a quality piece; radio reporters will want a few moments to conduct radio interviews and pick up sound effects. Leave enough time for everyone to get the material they need.

Provide plenty of background information and do your homework before-hand. You won't impress the journalists if you don't have the facts at your finger tips.

If you're planning a presentation or a formal ceremony as part of the facility visit don't be surprised if the journalists try and duck out of that part of the event. The more traditional local newspaper or freesheet may use photographs of presentations, but

Allow plenty of time and opportunity for journalists to get the shots and interviews they need.

to most journalists and photographers stilted speeches and people shaking hands are a waste of time. Concentrate on putting your message across by offering one-to-one interviews and interesting photo-opportunities.

Gimmicks

If you want the media to attend your event a good gimmick can help. Journalists will always look for the quirky, unusual angle in a story which will attract the audience's attention. Provide them with that ingredient and you double the chances of your event being covered. There are three secrets to the successful gimmick:

- keep it simple
- target it at your market
- the more unusual the better.

If. necessary, brain storm the options with friends or colleagues. Journalists are always attracted by the quirky or the unusual and they love the 'first', the 'biggest', the 'longest' and so on. If you're opening a new pizza shop create the 'Biggest Pizza in Britain'. It may be a gimmick and cost a little extra money, but the effort will be worth it if it attracts the coverage you want.

A computer company gained considerable publicity by establishing a new world record for Scalextric slot car racing. Eighty sets of the game were joined together to establish a course almost half a kilometre long, enough to get the company into the Guinness Book of Records. Afterwards the sets were given to staff as Christmas presents and the cost clawed back against tax as an advertising expense!

One games manufacturer achieved an extraordinary degree of interest by telephoning the local media with the news that a medium had been invited in to exorcise their factory. The company was launching a game supposedly invented by Henry VIII and it claimed a poltergeist had been hurling pieces of the game, shifting boxes and causing general mayhem around the factory. The media all *knew* it was a publicity stunt – but it was such a clever one they couldn't resist.

A good gimmick is quite irresistible to journalists.

Gimmicks can also be used to make a point forcefully in a crisis. For instance, if your job is to promote the efficacy of sewage treatment and the quality of bathing beaches, offering to take a well publicised swim at the coast will go a long way towards quelling any public doubts about your claims. But be careful not to leave hostages to fortune – your gimmick may backfire. When the issue of 'Mad Cow Disease' (BSE) first surfaced, the then Agriculture Minister John Gummer publicly defended the safety of British beef by feeding his daughter a beefburger in front of the cameras. At the time this was a simple yet powerful means of restoring public confidence. Later, when it emerged there *could* be a link between BSE and its human equivalent, CJD, Mr Gummer's action merely confirmed public fears that even the Government knew less about the situation than it claimed.

Become a 'media star'
One of the most effective ways to attract the attention of journalists to your cause is get your name into their contact books. If you acquire a reputation for giving good quotes and interesting, punchy interviews you will find the journalists will contact you every time they need a comment on a story in your field. You will have achieved the status of regular contributor. As the journalists come to know you, so you'll get to know them. The benefit for you is that the next time you want publicity you'll find it that much easier to interest the newsdesk because you will by then be on first name terms with at least some of the staff.

If you don't want to go this far, at least put some effort into establishing links with news editors and/or specialist reporters in your field. That way, instead of subjecting your story to the anonymous lottery of the newsroom selection process you just have to phone your contacts. They may well be grateful for your idea and run with it. If they don't, they'll explain why they don't want to, or can't, cover it. Don't be discouraged but try again next time with another idea.

5

HOW TO PREPARE FOR AN INTERVIEW

Once you have attracted the attention of the media you will at some stage be expected to give an interview. If you've never done one before this can be a hair raising prospect. Don't panic. There are several tips which will help you put your message across confidently and effectively.

The most important secret to handling interviews successfully is *preparation*. If you do your homework you will go into the interview in full command of the facts, confident that you know what to expect and with a clear idea of what you want to say and how to say it. If you allow yourself to be interviewed *without* thinking through what you want to say in advance you may leave out vital parts of your argument or you may find yourself saying things you will regret later. Also, if you don't find out beforehand what the interview involves and what will happen to it when it's finished you won't have any control over the direction the interview takes – total editorial control of the interview will be in the hands of the journalist!

Be assertive

It's important that you approach the interview in the correct frame of mind right from the start. There are two parties involved in an interview: you and the reporter. Although journalists might like to believe the opposite, *you* are the most important person in the interview. The reporter has come to you for information. You know something the reporter doesn't, otherwise s/he wouldn't be talking to you. That puts you in a position of power so make the most of it and don't let yourself be bullied. Too many people slavishly do what reporters ask of them without giving any thought to what they themselves want to get out of the interview. Be politely assertive from the minute you're contacted by the media.

Having said that, don't be unnecessarily aggressive or obstructive. If you put too many obstacles in the journalist's way s/he may become so irritated s/he may either drop the story altogether or adopt a more critical view of your position than might otherwise have been taken.

When the call comes, there are a number of things you will want to check before agreeing to the interview.

Things you need to know

Who's calling?

Establish the identity of the person you're talking to and the news organisation s/he represents. Most of the time the person will offer identification immediately without prompting and in the vast majority of cases s/he will be exactly who s/he claims to be. However, it's not unknown for investigative reporters to pretend to be somebody else if they think this will help them get information out of a reluctant interviewee. If you are the focus of media attention and you are trying to keep a story under wraps, be aware that journalists may use a number of ruses to get to the story. They may pretend to be from other parts of your company, or friends of friends, or they may claim to be from a news organisation they think you are more likely to trust than the one they actually represent. This sort of subterfuge is actually quite rare and it's unlikely to happen to you, but you should be aware that it can occur. If you have doubts about the identity of a caller, call back and check.

Which news organisation do they represent?

Knowing which news outlet you're talking to will give you a good guide to the sort of story the caller is pursuing and the way the story will be treated.

If you are contacted by a trade magazine or specialist journal in your field then the reporter will be looking for a story or angle which suits its defined audience.

National broadsheet newspapers like the *Times*, *Telegraph* and *Guardian* will be interested in a broad range of stories that will interest their readers, from kiss-and-tell scandal to complex and

sophisticated issues in science, business and politics. This also
applies to the major broadcasters such as the BBC and ITN.
Tabloid newspapers like the *Sun* and *Mirror* usually focus on
stories with a strong human element and preferably a degree of
controversy or scandal.

The tabloids have a reputation for dirt digging, sensationalism and inaccurate reporting, and certainly their approach to
news gathering is on occasion robust, to say the least. But –
and this may surprise you – the tabloids will often cover
more serious subjects with a high degree of accuracy, while the
more high-brow organs are not immune to the attractions of
sensationalism.

Locally based reporters are likely to be kinder to you than
those from the nationals because you're on their patch and they
may well need your goodwill again in the future.

What type of programme or article is the interview for?
If yours is a newspaper interview, establish whether it's a
'news' or 'feature' article. News stories focus on one clear cut
issue or event. They may well be reported by a journalist with
no expertise in your subject. Feature articles take a much
broader look at a range of issues or the background context to
a series of events. For instance, a news article might focus on
the formation of a neighbourhood watch scheme; a feature
article would look at such schemes in general, or perhaps the
whole issue of suburban crime prevention. Also, because of the
breadth of coverage, feature articles are usually researched in
more depth than news stories so the reporter may well be better
informed on the subject than his or her colleague who works
for news. If you're being interviewed for a feature article you
can anticipate a rather more searching line of questioning, but
often a fuller and fairer hearing.

If your interview is for radio or television you need to know
which programme, as different programmes will take different
approaches to a subject. A documentary programme is likely to
take a closer look at issues than a regional nightly magazine
programme. As with a feature writer, the documentary reporter is
likely to be better prepared and the question line more rigorous.
Hard hitting programmes such as *'The Cook Report'* take no
prisoners, so be prepared for a bumpy ride if you are the focus of
their attention.

What's the story?

You need to know the story the reporter is interested in and the angle s/he proposes to take. It's possible you might not be the best person to speak on the subject. A colleague may know more than you, and be a more appropriate interviewee. The reporter may have the wrong end of the stick; if so, you can put this right at the outset. For instance, if the reporter has heard on the grapevine that your company is laying off workers and that simply isn't true, now is the time to say so.

Most of the time journalists will be honest and explain what they think the story is and the particular line they're taking, but sometimes they may be less than open with you. This will occur particularly in the case of investigative programmes – the journalist may not want to reveal his or her hand too soon. Often journalists may not be too sure about the direction of the interview simply because, until they've spoken to you, they're not sure which avenues of enquiry may open up. This is an opportunity for you to clarify matters to your own advantage, either to kill the story if that's what you want to do, or to focus the reporter's attention towards the aspect of the story you wish to highlight.

Who else is being interviewed?

Check who else the reporter is speaking to. Journalists love controversy so if they can find someone with a view point opposed to yours they will do so. Knowing who else the journalist will speak to may influence what you want to say and the way that you say it. If your company is laying off workers the journalist will want to talk not just to you but also to the unions or the workers affected. However, don't assume the reporter will always seek an alternative viewpoint, especially if the story isn't controversial or the controversy is obscure. For instance, a reporter covering a story about a scientific discovery is unlikely to go to great lengths to find someone who disagrees with the principles of the discovery just for the sake of it.

Preparation

Insist on time to think

You should never go into an interview unprepared. There's no point in you allowing yourself to be rushed into an interview if that means you're not going to give of your best. Keep in mind that you're only giving an interview because you want to use the opportunity to put your message across to the public. That means knowing what you want to say and how you want to say it. Journalists are under constant time pressure – they live in a 'stop watch culture'. They will therefore try to persuade you to give instant comment. You may be prepared to do so, but if you feel you need a moment to marshal your thoughts, collect facts, talk to your press office (if you have one) or consult colleagues, then don't be afraid to ask for a little time before you give an interview. No reporter can seriously object to you taking half an hour or an hour to ensure your facts are correct and you know what you want to say. After all, it means you'll give a better interview! But play fair. Be aware that reporters have deadlines, and get back to them promptly. Telling a radio reporter you'll do an interview next week when s/he is looking to air the story in a hour's time is as good as saying "No comment". The chances are the reporter will run the story immediately but without your contribution.

Prepare your facts
Make sure you have all the facts to hand. If the details of your story are very familiar then this won't be a problem for you. If you are commenting on a complex issue, ensure you know the relevant information. If necessary make notes. Go back through your files to refresh your memory on things you may be unsure of. Think through likely questions which may be asked and prepare the facts you will need to give prompt and well informed answers.

Anticipate likely questions
You have every right to be told the general area of questioning, but no reporter will give you a detailed list of questions before the interview. An interview has been defined as 'a conversation with a purpose'. It should sound lively and spontaneous, each of your answers triggering a new and relevant question from the interviewer. If your interview is a combination of pre-prepared questions and scripted answers the result will sound very wooden and unconvincing.

Having said that, if you know the story the journalist is exploring, have a reasonable idea of the angle s/he is taking and also know the general area of questioning, you can take a good *guess* at what the questions will be.

The reporter's job is to get as much information out of you as possible. S/he may put you on the spot with specific so-called 'closed' questions – "Are you sacking staff or not?" – but mostly the questions will be 'open', and phrased in such a way that you can't answer simply 'yes' or 'no'. The most common open questions are just six in number:

What?
Why?
How?
Who?
When?
Where?

If your story is a 'good news story', the reporter may ask: *what* you're up to, *why* you're doing it, *how* you're doing it, and so forth.

If it's a bad news story and you're under attack, the question line will harden. *What*'s gone wrong? *Why? Who* was responsible? *What* are you doing to put matters right?

Predicting the broad thrust of the journalist's questions means you can prepare appropriate answers before the interview, when you've got time to think; the last thing you need during the interview is the added stress of an unexpected question. Think of an answer to the worst possible question you can imagine and everything else will be plain sailing!

Incidentally, if you *are* presented with a question which demands a yes or no answer be aware there's no rule which says you have to oblige. Inexperienced interviewees often cave in under this aggressive approach but the more seasoned campaigner will ignore the imperative in the question and say what s/he wants to say.

Many people think aggressive and penetrating interview technique is the norm in the media industry. This isn't so. The brusque and inquisitorial approach associated with the broadcaster Jeremy Paxman is actually quite rare. Most interviewers, especially local or regional journalists, will be much gentler with you.

Decide on what points you *want to put across*
Do not rely on the reporter to ask you questions which will allow you to make all your points. The reporter may want to focus on

one aspect of the situation which interests them, while you want to broaden the scope of the interview. There is no point in you giving an interview which is driven entirely by the journalist's own agenda. There will be points *you* want to make, so make a short-list of them and try and work those points into your answers during the interview. Too often, ill-prepared interviewees only think of pertinent points they should have made *after* the interview – when it's too late.

Be prepared to distil your arguments down. In the average radio or TV interview you will only have time for two or three key points. You'll have more leeway if you are taking part in a longer discussion programme or newspaper interview but even then time is limited, so work out the main points you want to make and be ruthless in abandoning unnecessary detail.

Brief the reporter
Don't assume the journalist knows the background to your story. The nature of news is such that the reporter who interviews you will have had little time to prepare; s/he will be working from what information s/he's been able to glean from a press release, newspaper cutting or, in some cases, an official report or council agenda. If you don't make sure the reporter knows what the story is about – and correct any misconceptions – you have only yourself to blame if the final report is wrong or unsatisfactory. Another advantage of briefing the reporter properly is that you may sway him or her to your point of view. If your story is controversial and you are first on the reporter's list of people to see, a convincing exposition of your view may help to influence the reporter with your 'spin' on the facts.

Giving a background briefing need not take long. In fact, if you go into too much detail you'll simply confuse the journalist. Stick to the essential information s/he needs to understand the story. If you've contacted the paper or the station for publicity, outline what you're up to and why, who's involved and other essential relevant information. If the journalist has approached you for comment, state your position clearly and give essential background information the reporter may be able to use.

If there are things you don't want the reporter to know, keep quiet. By all means prepare answers to these points in case they are raised by the journalist but if not, don't put your own head on the block by bringing up such points yourself.

Off the record

'Off the record' is a device by which the interviewee gives the journalist confidential background information which will help in the preparation of a story, but which is not itself intended for publication or broadcast. 'Off the record' briefings can be useful, especially to politicians who may want to influence media coverage of an issue without compromising their own position by 'going public'. For most people it's a dangerous tool. The safest approach to an interview is to assume all you say will be reported. Unless you really know and trust the reporter never say anything which could cause serious damage if it ever got out.

If you *do* go off the record don't alternate between 'on' and 'off' the record – the journalist may forget which is which. Also, be aware that reporters have a number of sources. It's entirely possible they may be able to confirm your 'off the record' briefing with a third party who is willing to make the information public. This will enable the journalist to publish the information you gave them without technically breaking your confidence.

Putting yourself in the right frame of mind for an interview is important. Prepare what you want to say and anticipate likely questions, insist on knowing everything you need to know about the interview before-hand and take the trouble to brief the reporter. But what can you expect in the interview itself? What do you need to watch out for? How can you put your points across effectively? These questions will be answered in the next three chapters which look at press, radio and television interviews in more detail.

6

HOW TO HANDLE A PRESS INTERVIEW

In some respects the press interview is the simplest of all interviews to handle. There is none of the technical paraphernalia of radio or television, just a reporter clutching a notebook or small tape recorder to record your conversation and perhaps a photographer with a stills camera. However, the press interview can cause interviewees more headaches than any other form of media encounter.

This is because there are more opportunities for error in a press interview. What you say in the radio and television interview is (more or less) what will be transmitted; in a newspaper interview you're dependent on the professionalism and integrity of the reporter to quote you accurately and not distort what you say. If you haven't briefed them properly reporters may misunderstand the story, and if they can't read their shorthand they may invent quotes you didn't give. The potential for error doesn't end there. When the draft story leaves the reporter it goes to a sub-editor who fits the words to the page and in the process crucial parts of your argument may be abbreviated or dropped altogether.

Undoubtedly, errors and distortion can occur from time to time but professional press officers who work with the print media on a daily basis agree the benefits of talking to newspapers outweigh the occasional disadvantages.

How will the interview be conducted – and what should I watch out for?
The press interview is carried out in one of two ways: the reporter will either come to see you in person or s/he will carry out a telephone interview.

If the interview is short it may well be conducted over the

telephone. Be aware that many newspapers have the facility to record telephone conversations. What you say may not be quoted in its entirety but there is a possibility that casual comments may be picked up and used.

If the interview is carried out in your home or office you must realise the reporter's most important recording equipment is not the notebook or tape machine but his or her eyes, ears and brain. The interview doesn't start when the notebook opens or the tape recorder is switched on. The reporter will have been mentally recording impressions, even usable quotes, from the minute s/he stepped through your door. Nor does the interview finish when the notebook is closed or the recorder is switched off. Be on your guard from the minute you meet the reporter and don't relax until the reporter has gone. Some of the best quotes often come from a passing shot at the door. A chance remark made 'off the cuff' could very well find its way into the published article.

Newspaper interviews are often more relaxed than their broadcast counterparts as there is no need for a 'performance' for the camera or microphone. But be careful not to relax too much, especially if the reporter appears sympathetic and caring. Not all journalists are heartless and manipulative; more than a few often become genuinely moved by and involved in the stories they cover. But be wary, particularly if your story is harrowing or you are under pressure. You may over-react to a proffered sympathetic shoulder and spill more beans than you should. Treat every contact with a journalist as an interview, whether it's a formal discussion in your office or a chat in a pub.

"Between you 'n' me . . ."
While we're on the subject of pubs, beware the demon drink! Fourth pint confessions can easily find their way into print the next morning. Also, if you're discussing a sensitive issue in a public place like a bar or restaurant be careful you don't impart confidences which may be overheard by the wrong people. One reporter I know scooped an important story about the downfall of a computer company because he chanced to overhear a conversation between two of the company's directors in a restaurant.

Tricks of the trade and how to deal with them
In the interview itself, the reporter may say very little, merely nodding occasionally or throwing in the odd short question:

Be careful about discussing sensitive issues in public places.

'why?' or 'and?'. This could mean s/he finds what you say absolutely riveting. It can also be a clever ruse to encourage you to say
more than you mean to. I was once interviewed by a Romanian
journalist who asked no questions at all – I was merely invited to
talk. The temptation to unburden the soul was overwhelming and
potentially very awkward if I had said the wrong thing. Watch what
you say and remember your meandering may yield a rich seam of
quotes when the reporter reviews the interview later. If the reporter
is the silent type, don't say more than you mean to and stick to your
main arguments. Remember, you're only doing the interview
because you want to use the opportunity to say what *you* want to the
public, in this case readers of the particular newspaper. Don't feel
you have to persuade the reporter that s/he should like you or your
arguments. You may find you're saying too much in an unconscious
bid to win approval or agreement.

Alternatively, the reporter may hog the interview. S/he may
say a great deal, thereby reducing your contribution to a series of

nods and grunts. In radio or television such responses would be unusable; in a newspaper interview they may be taken to indicate your agreement with what the reporter has suggested and written up as an actual quote. For instance, if the reporter says "If I were in your shoes, I'd cut back on the workforce to stay competitive" and you nod without thinking or don't firmly disagree with the assumption in the question, you may be somewhat surprised to find yourself quoted as saying jobs must go if you are to stay in business. If you're faced with the verbose reporter, don't be afraid to butt in. Don't grunt or nod or give other throwaway responses which may be taken as confirmation of the reporter's comment. Give comprehensive answers which can't be misconstrued.

Be suspicious of the light hearted approach. It is entirely possible the journalist is being genuinely friendly with no ulterior motive. On the other hand, it might be a cunning ploy to lull you into a false sense of security. If the story the journalist is investigating could have negative implications for you or your organisation, be certain the journalist will draw those implications out. If allegations are put to you in a flip or nonchalant way, make sure you treat the points seriously and give comprehensive answers.

Always meet a negative question with a positive reply. Never be browbeaten into agreeing with the negative assumption in the interviewer's question. There is usually at least something you can say which puts a positive spin on the situation.

Deadlines

Daily newspapers have to work to strict deadlines, but weekly papers and magazines usually have more flexibility. Some newspaper and magazine interviews therefore last longer than their radio and television equivalents. A complicated feature article may require an interview which takes up several hours or even a day in extreme cases. At the other end of the scale the reporter may just want a quote as a follow up to your press release, which will hardly take any time at all. Magazines often work well ahead of the publication date – several months in some cases. While this distant deadline makes it less imperative that you give an instant response to the reporter it also means you should be careful to say what will be relevant in the *future*. Don't leave hostages to fortune, they may come back to haunt you.

Watch your back

Consider making an independent recording of the interview. Take a small tape recorder or dictaphone into the interview and place it near you for the duration of the conversation. No responsible reporter should mind you doing so and it will be useful in two ways. It will impress the reporter you mean business and may discourage them from being cavalier with their interpretation of your comments. An independent recording will also provide you with back up if you are misquoted in a way which causes you trouble. If you have your own record of the interview you can prove your innocence; if you haven't, it's your word against the reporter's.

The photographer

A picture, they say, is worth a thousand words. In fact, if the story is photogenic but otherwise boring, a photograph with caption may be all that's published. Don't worry, it's still good publicity. An eye catching photograph may well be run across several columns in the newspaper or magazine, attracting more public interest than if the same story had been written up as a small piece of copy. So welcome the presence of a photographer. Go out of your way to point him or her towards what you think might make good pictures, though don't try to dictate what should be photographed and how, and don't be disappointed if s/he finds something else to photograph which is more suitable. For instance, if you're manufacturing a spray to keep pigs cool in summer you might think a close up photograph of your invention would be adequate. But a good press photographer will want to shoot pigs using the spray, or you scrubbing a pig's back under the spray, or any one of a number of creative alternatives. Unless you think the photographer's aim is to make you look foolish or denigrate your product, go along with any suggestions; appreciate the fact that you've got a professional working for you and it's not costing you a penny.

Some people worry that photographers will try and present them in a bad light, perhaps by taking their picture in front of a backdrop which would put the lie to what they say in the interview. Such fears are nearly always groundless; it's only top politicians who suffer from photographers' attempts to take them down a peg, and then only at election time. But a good photographer will be aware of his or her surroundings and their photographic and news potential, so do glance over your shoulder before your picture is taken. If you're defending the quality of effluent emissions from your factory and you are photographed in front of a graph clearly showing a rise in pollution the reader could be forgiven for disbelieving what you say. If there's confidential material in your office which you don't want the photographer and reporter to see put it away before they arrive.

If you want to influence the type of photograph used, or if you know the reporter won't bring a photographer along, it may be a good idea to have your own photographs available to give out. It's worth having these taken professionally unless you are a skilled amateur; a fuzzy snapshot is unlikely to get published and won't do you and your product or project any good if it is – a sharp, attractive image is more likely to succeed. If you're supplying a newspaper, offer black and white or colour prints at least 18 × 12cm (7″ × 5″) or larger. Magazines will be able to use colour slides (35mm or larger) but they will be even more fussy about the quality of the image than newspapers, so only offer the best pictures you can provide.

Never a borrower nor lender be . . .
If a newspaper or magazine wants to borrow a valuable or irreplaceable photograph or other material from you for copying be very careful. If it's in your interests to let them have the material then do so, but be aware things can easily get lost in busy news rooms. Reporters and photographers tend to rapidly forget the commitments they have made while covering a story once they've moved on to a new project. If you can, insist that anything they want to use be copied by photographing it in your office or home.

If you do let your treasure out of your sight, impress on the reporter or photographer its value to you and threaten them with the fear of God if it's lost. Make contact promptly after the story is finished to find out where it's got to. Don't leave things, assuming the paper will be in touch. Any delay will increase the chances of your property being mislaid.

What come back do I have?
Once the interview is over and the reporter and photographer have gone you have little say in how the story is written up. It is possible that a reporter may read his or her 'copy' through to you

if you phone and ask to 'vet' the finished article. Trade magazines, in particular, will be happy for you to check what they've
written in this way, but it is unlikely that a national tabloid
newspaper would be so co-operative! Newspaper journalists guard
their editorial independence as jealously as do journalists from any
other medium. Having said that, a little basic psychology may
help. As the reporter leaves, politely suggest you are happy to
check his or her copy if s/he is unsure about anything. If the issue is
complex the reporter may well take you up on your offer.

If you are unhappy with the final result there are a number of
options. If the error is minor then it's best to shrug your shoulders
and forget it. No editor will offer you a published apology or
retraction for a small factual error or dispute over interpretation,
though s/he may accept a letter for publication – particularly if
your complaint is itself controversial or colourful! If the mistake
is serious then contact the reporter and point this out. S/he may
not be able to do anything about the story which has already been
published, but it should be possible to correct the newspaper's
files so the same mistake isn't repeated if the story is re-used in
another context in future. If you get no satisfaction from the
reporter then contact the news editor. An apology or retraction
may be offered, especially if the mistake is sufficiently serious
for you to have grounds for legal action against the paper.

If the error is very serious, or your complaint relates to a
breach of privacy, then contact the Press Complaints Commission. This body exists to discipline the print media, though an
adjudication in your favour is unlikely to give you more than
passing satisfaction.

Finally, if your company holds a major advertising account
with a newspaper don't assume this will necessarily give you the
power to veto a story which reflects badly on you or the
company. Of course, it's a wicked world and the fact that you
play golf with the newspaper's proprietor could work in your
favour, but usually newspaper journalists will firmly resist any
attempt to manipulate their news judgement. However, the proprietor or advertising manager can be a useful ally in some
circumstances. If you're getting little coverage for your story, ask
why before you place your next large advertising order. Subtlety
is what you need here. Bullying won't work, but if your story is
newsworthy a little judicious 'leaning' on the right people may
achieve the publicity you seek.

7

HOW TO HANDLE A BROADCAST INTERVIEW

The secret of being effective in a broadcast interview is knowing what to expect and what you want to say. You need to find out as much as possible about the interview before-hand. If you are clear about what's required of you, and you know what to expect in the interview, you're more likely to be confident and give a good account of yourself.

What's the subject of the interview?
What's the story? Usually the journalist will be happy to tell you. It may be you're not the right person to speak to, or a colleague may be better qualified to give the interview. Sometimes the journalist may be less than open about the story and the angle s/he is taking. This can be because the subject is sensitive and the reporter doesn't want to alert you to the real issue of interest or it may be because the subject is complex and the reporter still isn't sure where his or her research is leading.

Will the interview be live or pre-recorded?
If the interview is transmitted live the advantage to you is that everything you say will go out unedited. On the other hand, a live interview may require you to be at a studio at an inconvenient time of day or night and it can also be more stressful. A pre-recorded interview may be manipulated by the journalist but it is usually easier to fit a 'pre-record' into your schedule and it can always be repeated if you make an important mistake.

Who else is taking part?
Are you the sole interviewee or one of a number? Who else is the

interviewer talking to? If you are being asked to give information on a non-controversial subject, or if you are passing expert comment, you will be on your own. If the subject is controversial, expect the programme to interview others with an opposing or alternative viewpoint to your own. Ask who those people are. This will give you an idea of what points to prepare for the interview.

How much airtime will I have?
If it's a live interview you need to know how long you will have on air. If it's short (around three minutes) you need to be very clear and focused on the essential points you want to get across. If it's an extended interview of up to an hour you will need to be well prepared with facts to enable you to sustain an interesting discussion for that long.

Where and when will the interview be used?
If it's pre-recorded you will want to know when the interview material will be broadcast so you can watch or record the finished result! You will also want to know where it will be shown or played. BBC stations in particular swap material that may be of interest to other regions; material is also exchanged between local and national stations. If you're doing an interview for a provincial station don't assume it won't be heard elsewhere in the country, couch your arguments accordingly and don't say something you may regret if it's heard by a wider or different audience.

How is the material to be used?
A pre-recorded interview may stand alone as what's known as a *'head to head'*. As the name implies, the interview is transmitted in the same form it was recorded, that is, as a series of questions and answers. It may go out 'warts and all' or it may be lightly edited for cosmetic reasons. Usually the first question is dropped from a head to head interview and included in the written *'cue'*, or introduction, which a programme presenter will use to preface your interview: ''Our reporter spoke to councillor Bill Brown and asked him how the policy would work . . .''

Cue [Answer Question Answer Question Answer]

If the reporter wants to include a number of different points of view in a short time span, s/he may work your interview into a *package*. Single answers (called *clips*, or *sound bites*) are taken from a series of interviews with different interviewees and then linked together by a script written by the reporter.

Cue [Script Answer 1 Script Answer 2 Script]

The 'sound bite'

You would be forgiven for asking just how much an audience can learn about an issue when all it knows of the subject is summed up in a 30 or 40 second sound bite. The conspiracy theorists warn that the sound bite is a perfect vehicle for beguiling the public into thinking it is being informed and consulted on a situation while actually keeping people more or less completely in the dark.

Whatever it's broader implications for society and freedom of information, the sound bite is a by-product of the way the electronic media work. Air time is limited so issues can't be explored in the same depth as is possible in a detailed newspaper article. The average news bulletin is just three minutes long. If the audience is to get a rounded view of the latest stories, it is necessary to pack several of them into that small time span. That means each story gets thirty seconds or less. The same limitation applies to longer news programmes. The whole programme may last half an hour or more, but the programme's producer will try and cram as many as ten stories into that time. Some will be brief mentions of minor stories – so-called 'News in Brief', or NIBs for short – but even more important stories may receive only two to three minutes of airtime. Also, to ensure balanced coverage it may be necessary to include two or more viewpoints. If all relevant facts and opinions are to be included each individual view point will, inevitably, be limited to less than a minute.

Another reason for the popularity of the sound bite on some channels is the limit of the audience's attention span. Long and involved discussions of issues may have their place in highbrow extended news programmes but these are watched by a minority. Most viewers watch only the mainstream TV news bulletins, many radio listeners listen only to short, hourly, news bulletins – and then with half an ear. It's difficult for any listener or viewer to fully understand extended and detailed coverage of complex subjects when s/he is swept along by the programme and has no opportunity to pause and mull over the finer points of its content.

Highly experienced communicators, including most senior politicians, recognise the importance of the sound bite. They will hone down their arguments to the point where they may not give full interviews at all. Presented with a camera or microphone they will deliver a short 'potted' summary of their view or position and that will be that. Such a brief media encounter saves everyone time and ensures that the interviewee maintains control over what is transmitted. If the sound bite is strong, concise, interesting and to the point it will be transmitted uncut. A long rambling interview will have to be edited to extract the pithy summary required – and that puts editorial control of your message firmly in the hands of the journalist!

Learning to give the media well crafted sound bites is a useful skill. How do you do it?

The sound bite should be *self-contained*. Often the question which generated an answer in your interview will be dropped in the broadcast version. This means there's a risk that what you say could be taken out of context. A self contained answer is one which includes the central point of the question, making it much more difficult for your reply to be misinterpreted. For instance, if I ask you what you had for breakfast you might reply "Toast", but if I use your answer without the question I could, if I wanted, make you say you *hate* "Toast". The self-contained answer "I had toast for breakfast" avoids this problem. If you self-contain your answers in this way you will not only sound more authoritative and professional, you also minimise the chances that the interview will be changed by a mischievous journalist; the journalist can't alter the meaning of your answer without physically cutting the tape on which your answer is recorded.

Second, decide whether to concentrate on one key point in your sound bite or, alternatively, use the opportunity to summarise two or three key points;

Q: "Why are you campaigning for a new by-pass?"
A: "This village must have a new by-pass because sooner or later someone is going to die. We have already had three bad accidents in less than six months. Unless something is done, and done soon, we will have a death on our hands. And then it will be too late!"

Or: "This village must have a new by-pass now. We have already had three bad accidents in less than six months, and sooner or later someone is going to die. The sheer volume of traffic is damaging high street property, and the village is hopelessly split because it's often impossible to cross the road."

Third, end with a bang – either a key demand or a solution to the problem you've outlined. This will neatly end the sound bite and leave your last comment ringing in the ears of the audience.

Q: "Why are you campaigning for a new by-pass?"
A: "This village must have a new by-pass because sooner or later someone is going to die. We have already had three bad accidents in less than six months. Unless something is done, and done soon, we will have a death on our hands. And then it will be too late. If work starts now, the by-pass could be finished in less than a year, and that would remove for ever the fear that it's our children's blood which will stain the tarmac in front of our homes!"

Dramatic perhaps, but if that's the campaigners' message then that's the way to put it across – grab the audience by the heart strings and get them involved in the story.

Although short – just five sentences long – this sound bite efficiently sums up the campaigners' argument. If you read it out, you'll find it lasts just 23 seconds. The ideal length for a sound bite is between 15 and 30 seconds.

Crafting sound bites is a skill which improves with practice and you don't need to acquire that experience on air. Try it in your office or home. Take a subject, think through what you want to say and condense that message down to a few sentences, then deliver it confidently, crisply and concisely.

Your place or mine
Where the interview takes place is subject to the programme's requirements and your convenience.

If the story involves interesting things to film or sounds to record, then expect to be asked if the interview can be recorded where the action is. If the story is about your new factory process or your award winning sunflower, the television viewer will expect to see what you're talking about. The interview will mean little if you're interviewed in your living room and the subject of your conversation is sitting out of sight in the front flower bed. In the same way, radio listeners will want to hear sounds relevant to the interview, so expect the radio reporter to seek out a location with appropriate ambient noises.

On the other hand, some subjects don't lend themselves to any particular location. If you're talking about something nebulous like a policy issue or commenting on something which is happening far away it doesn't really matter where you are interviewed. In this case the interview will take place in your front room or office, or in a studio (either live or pre-recorded). For more on this topic see Chapters 9 and 10.

Brief the reporter
Before the interview be sure to have a chat with the interviewer. It's in your interest to make sure s/he is as well briefed on the story as possible. Talk the story through. Don't bore the reporter with too much detail, but do satisfy yourself s/he has a reasonable idea of what the story is all about.

If it is a live radio interview you will have little chance to speak with the interviewer before-hand; s/he will be working from a briefing script provided by the producer or researcher who first invited you to take part in the programme. Ensure the producer or researcher has enough information to brief the interviewer adequately.

Prepare what you want to say
Although radio and television interviews are rarely longer than three minutes (and may be even shorter), if you prepare what you want to say you can pack quite a few positive messages into the short time available. But this preparation must take place before the interview.

Decide in advance what you want to say – and make sure you say it! There's no point whatsoever in a bright idea which occurs to you as you leave the studio. Distil your argument down to two or three main points and then find an opportunity to squeeze them into your answers.

Prepare for likely questions
You will never persuade a journalist to give you a list of questions but you can always predict the sort of thing s/he will ask: who, what, why, how, when and where? There may also be

specific questions related to the subject. Usually, you can expect a more informed question line from a specialist correspondent, but don't assume s/he will be fully *au fait* with your arguments; sometimes the key questions are the simple ones and the specialist can be too clever for their own good, or s/he may pretend to have more knowledge than is the case. Decide before the interview what the questions are likely to be and prepare suitable answers. Even if the precise question you anticipated doesn't arise in the interview you may be able to use your prepared material to answer a similar question.

Putting your arguments across
This is the central and most important part of the interview. If you don't put your arguments across effectively there will have been no point in you doing the interview in the first place.

Treat the questions as prompts
Try to answer the question. Politicians often don't, but this can be very irritating for the audience. Baroness Thatcher was an arch-exponent of the art. In response to a direct question she would reply "That's a very interesting point, but the real issue is . . ." and take the interview off in a direction of her own choosing. Address the question, but make sure you say what you want to say as well. Treat the question as a spring board from which to take the argument off in your own chosen direction. But don't try to avoid awkward but important questions by taking the conversation too far off beam – you'll simply sound ridiculous.

Keep your answers simple
If you say something obtuse or difficult to understand in a newspaper interview, the reader can sit and puzzle out your meaning until s/he understands it. In radio and television the audience only has one chance to grab your message, and that's when it goes out. The viewer and listener can't spend time working out what it is you're trying to say, they will either lose interest completely or miss the thread of your argument.

Keep your answers concise
You don't have long to say what you want to say on radio and television so keep your answers crisp and short – around three to four sentences is a good average length for each point. And don't

grumble on air about the lack of time you have, it will simply waste *more* time!

Another good reason to keep your answers concise is that it helps you increase your control over what is broadcast from a pre-recorded interview. If you waffle, the journalist will be forced to cut your interview down to the required length and the decision on what to cut and what to leave in will be taken by the journalist. If you talk for five minutes and only two minutes of airtime is available, sixty percent of your interview – well over half – will be ditched. If, on the other hand, your interview is around two minutes long, the chances are the whole interview will be broadcast uncut.

Make your answers self-contained
As we have seen in the section on sound bites earlier in this chapter, including the premise of the question in each of your answers will make them sound more authoritative and it will help minimise the possibility of the reporter changing the meaning of what you say.

Keep your answers concise and to the point.

Avoid trying to be funny . . . unless you are!
A good gag cracked at the right point of an interview may have your audience rolling in the aisles. The jolly accountant and wise cracking cleric are wonderful when they work, but be very sure you're as funny as you think you are – you may simply end up sounding foolish.

Avoid jargon
We all develop our own private language to communicate with others within the family, a trade or a profession. The problem comes when we use specialist words and concepts to talk to people who don't understand them.

Jargon isn't a problem if you're being interviewed for a specialist trade magazine in your field. Both the journalist and the audience will grasp your meaning because they're in the same line of business but a mass radio or television audience won't understand jargon. As what you say goes in one ear and out the other in a broadcast interview, it's vital the listener or viewer doesn't have to struggle to follow your meaning.

There are three types of jargon, all of which should be avoided when addressing a general audience.

Word jargon
Many professions and trades generate specialist terms and acronyms which mean something to their members but not to others. This is particularly true of the sciences. Unless you're a doctor it's not obvious that a *myocardial infarct* is a heart attack or that *in vitro fertilisation* is a test tube baby, and no-one but an environmental scientist would know that IPC stands for *Integrated Pollution Control*.

The secret to avoiding word jargon is to substitute everyday terms everyone understands for specialist words, and explain in everyday terms jargon you do let slip through or can't avoid. Before the interview, think through what you want to say and try to work out everyday alternatives before you need them so they then trip off the tongue in the interview itself. One way to reach the right level of communication is to visualise your viewer or listener as a ten year old child. This will encourage you to use simple terms. Don't worry about patronising the audience, but don't talk as if you were addressing an infants' class. Sarcasm never works, and may rebound on you.

Another tip which may help you avoid word jargon is to use 'picture words'. Words evoke images in the mind. If we can't visualise the object of a word we have to think about its meaning and that takes time – a luxury the TV viewer or radio listener doesn't have. For instance, understanding 'in vitro fertilisation' means working out what the words in the phrase mean before we can grasp what the term implies. The everyday alternative phrase 'Test tube baby' immediately evokes a mental image which the audience can understand without struggling. Similarly, 'abstraction' is a technical term frequently used in the water industry. It's not easy to visualise 'abstraction'; the alternative term 'taking water out' is simple to understand.

Concept jargon
Some concepts are so alien to the general public that even if you use simple terms to explain them, the *ideas* you're trying to put across may be too complicated to understand. This is a particular problem for scientists. If you are an astronomer trying to explain the birth of the universe, putting your ideas across can be difficult when the average member of the public has only the haziest idea of the difference between a star and a planet.

If you think you may have a problem with explaining a complex idea, stop and ponder. Is there a simple everyday *example* or *analogy* which will help? Relating the idea you're trying to communicate to a commonplace concept which will be familiar to the audience will help them understand what you're trying to say. I once interviewed a famous astronomer about his theory on how galaxies formed. To help the audience grasp the concept he used the analogy of sweeping autumn leaves into bigger and bigger clumps which were then burnt in a bonfire; not technically rigorous, perhaps, but it helped the audience to visualise what he was talking about.

Do not expect inspiration to strike during the interview. If you think you will need examples, analogies – even anecdotes – to put your point across, invent them before-hand.

'Official speak'
A third type of jargon which bedevils civil servants and bureaucrats in particular is Procedural Jargon. If procedures and decisions are important to your work you'll feel you need to talk about them, but remember the audience won't want to hear the

technical details. They just want to know the end result. So avoid going into detailed explanations of procedures unless they're vital to your argument.

Avoid using euphemisms which are clearly intended to distract the audience from the real significance of your story. For instance, if you're making staff redundant, talking about 'down-sizing' or 'restructuring' will fool no-one and may alienate many in your audience.

Statistics
Numbers are difficult for the audience to grasp in a broadcast interview, so unless the exact figure is crucial to your argument, round the number up or down. For example, '1,256,789' means something if you see it written down, but not if you hear it just once on radio or television. 'One and a quarter million' is much easier for the audience to visualise.

Percentages are also easier for the audience to understand if you generalise. 'One third' creates a clear mental image in the listener's mind – '34.5%' doesn't.

Interviewer's tricks
Most broadcast interviews do not involve a grand inquisition. The purpose is simply to find out more about a situation for the education, information and perhaps entertainment of the listening public. The interviewer's questions may be little more than prompts, intended to tease information out of you. But if things have gone wrong the interviewer will feel the need to put you on the spot and ask more probing questions, to find out what happened or to test the strength of your arguments.

If you are under attack from the interviewer, don't be brow-beaten. Stand your ground. A spirited display of resistance may be enough to turn the edge of awkward questions.

Different interviewers adopt different styles depending on their personality, the nature of the programme and who's being inter-viewed. You will very likely come across one or more of the following.

The 'rottweiler'
This is the aggressive, adversarial frontal attack. The interviewer may exaggerate or distort the seriousness of the situation to extract a spirited response. Questions may be hard and pointed:

"So your policy is a failure then?''. The interviewer may deliberately distort your own arguments to confuse you or demonstrate the weakness of your position. The interview may verge on a personal attack in an effort to make you appear foolish. A key question may be repeated to wear you down into giving the required answer.

This adversarial style of interview will be familiar to politicians, lawyers and academics, all professions where close and sometimes aggressive questioning are common within the professional structure itself. It may come as more of a shock to others who aren't used to a comparative stranger giving them a hard time.

There are a number of tips which will help you face the aggressive interviewer.

Stay cool. Don't lose your temper, and never storm out of the interview. In either case you will be seen to have lost the argument.

Be assertive. Don't be overawed by the interviewer. Remember s/he is only flesh and blood, like you. Don't go on the defensive and resort to short answers which strictly address the question, it will appear as if every point the interviewer makes is finding its mark. Explain your position fully and set your own pace. Not only will you appear to be in command of the situation but the more you say the more *your* point of view will be recollected by the audience.

Be prepared. The interviewer knows less than you about your subject, so the chances are the questions will have factual or conceptual weaknesses. If you have the facts at your fingertips you will be able to quash any provocative question with a reasoned answer. If you're uncertain about the finer points of your argument then the likelihood is you will appear uninformed and defensive. As your confidence wanes, so will the strength of your argument.

By all means challenge the interviewer's knowledge of the subject, but be careful, s/he may be better informed than you think and may turn the tables and make mincemeat of your argument. Also, remember you're talking through the interviewer to the audience, and the viewers and listeners may not be too impressed by your attitude. Trying to make the interviewer look foolish is usually a mistake, especially in the case of a prerecorded interview as s/he will simply cut out those parts of your interview before transmission.

If you disagree with an assumption in the question, say so. Don't let the point pass without comment, it may seem as if you endorse it. Similarly, avoid appearing to agree to a point made in the question even though you are going on to disagree with it. Faced with the sort of question which starts "Some people are concerned that . . ." or "Some people might say that . . .", the natural response is to reply "Yes", to acknowledge the point made, before going on to argue against it. Be wary. Shorn of the rest of your answer this apparent agreement can be taken out of context.

Be positive. Always meet negative questions with positive answers. This may take some thought, so preparation before the interview is essential – don't expect inspiration to strike in the middle of a heated exchange. If your reply to the question "So your policy is a failure?" is "Well, I suppose it may seem like that", you will have dug yourself into a hole from which it may be difficult to extricate yourself. A much stronger and more positive answer would be "On the contrary, the policy has been a glowing success, because . . ." If necessary refer to the failure, but only *after* you have highlighted the successes.

Stick to your guns. The interviewer may repeat a question in a bid to elicit a particular answer. If this happens to you, turn the tables on the interviewer by repeating your answer until s/he gets bored or runs out of time. Don't be bullied into changing your reply. Having said that, it's important to realise the repeated question may not always be an attempt to torpedo your set response. The reporter may think that you have not put your answer very well and the repeated question is simply a device to get you to improve your reply. Judge the situation on its merits.

The 'pussy cat'

Like the animal of that ilk, this type of interviewer relies more on stealth than outright aggression to extract the information or answer he or she wants. The interviewer will ask you 'open' questions which are designed to tease information out of you. By listening closely to the answers and tailoring subsequent questions to suit s/he can ease you towards a precipice of their own choosing which it's hoped you won't see until too late. The *coup de gras* often comes after a dramatic pause: "So what you've just said is that your policy is a failure after all!"

If you are to cope effectively with this technique you will need to be as devious as the interviewer. Think through potential pitfalls before the interview and if you spot yourself being pushed towards one, take action. Move the conversation off in another direction or pre-empt the interviewer's final attack by tackling the point yourself and putting your own 'spin' on it.

The 'fool'

You may come across the interviewer, very possibly a presenter with no journalistic background, who has no knowledge of your subject and no interest in it. This can be frustrating but there is a way of turning this type of interview to your advantage.

Don't patronise the interviewer or make it obvious you think their questions stupid or ill-informed. Bear in mind why you're doing the interview and stick to the points you want to make, correcting wrong assumptions in the questions where necessary. The presenter's approach no doubt suits that particular audience, so take his or her attitude as a clue to how you should tackle your subject. Stick to simple explanations, explain complicated ideas using everyday examples and analogies and spell out your points in as simple a way as possible. That way you will achieve successful communication with an audience which may not be to your choosing, but which is better than none at all.

Be aware that the apparent 'fool' can be a variant of the 'pussy cat'. A finely honed mind may be hidden by the seemingly banal facade and you may realise your peril too late.

Never trust a microphone or camera

As a rule studio staff and interviewers will not try and catch you out by recording what you say without your knowledge but accidents can happen. Always assume a microphone or camera is live and never ever say anything you may regret when near one – it's just possible what you say may be recorded or actually transmitted. Former US president Ronald Reagan once famously answered a request for a pre-interview sound level check by announcing he was going to bomb Russia in five minutes time! Make sure you're not the unwitting subject of the latest story.

Coping with upsets

Calming the butterflies

You are sure to be nervous before a broadcast interview. There seems to be so much to think about. Will I remember to make all my points? Will the presenter ask me awkward questions? Have I missed anything out? If the interview is live you may also be acutely aware that you're about to talk to thousands, perhaps millions, of people. The end result can be butterflies in the stomach, a sudden desire to visit the loo, a dry mouth and rising panic.

The first thing to realise is that everyone is nervous before interviews. Broadcasters are subject to butterflies too. In fact, some degree of nervous tension is a good thing. The adrenalin flowing through your system can sharpen your responses and put a cutting edge on your performance which would be missing if you were too laid back.

But you won't give of your best if you become *too* nervous. If the butterflies threaten to choke you then it's time to look at ways of calming down.

The first answer to excessive nerves is preparation. If you go into an interview unsure of what's involved, without preparing what you want to say and without the facts at your finger tips, you are sure to come a cropper. If you hope for the best, the best won't happen. Do your homework in advance. Make sure you find out before-hand everything you need to know about the interview. Prepare for likely questions. Think through any illustrations, quips or examples you may want to use and prepare yourself to translate any jargon you feel you may be tempted to use. That way, when you're waiting for the interview to start you'll be as confident as you can be that you'll be ready for all eventualities.

The second tip for calming nerves is to distract your mind. 'Nerves' are a symptom of the body's need to handle stress in such a way as to avoid what it thinks is a looming crisis – the so-called 'flight or fight' syndrome. Hopefully you won't be indulging in either flight or fight in the interview so your body has no way of relieving the growing stress level. Try and calm the mind by giving it something to do. Former BBC voice trainer Nick Willmot suggests the following.

- Breathe slowly and consciously to a count. Inhale until your lungs are full. Hold the breath for a second and then exhale steadily. Count 'one'. Then repeat. Each cycle should last around ten seconds. You will find an immediate calming affect.

Calm nerves with deep breathing exercises.

- Visualise a balloon slowly descending from the ceiling. Imagine it gently drifting down to the floor or table in front of you. Again, the mind will be distracted from its instinctive desire to panic and you should find your breathing and thought processes calming down.
- Take an interest in what's going on around you. If you can put yourself in a frame of mind which accepts the interview as a chance to do something different in unusual surroundings, you'll be on your way to enjoying the experience. It's certainly preferable to treating the whole exercise as one step worse than a visit to the dentist. But don't get so distracted you forget the need to concentrate on the interview!

What if I freeze?
Some people worry about 'freezing' in an interview, particularly if it's live. Even experienced broadcasters suddenly find the mind goes blank at some point. Don't worry if this happens to you. If you dry up, the presenter will rescue you. S/he will recognise the

symptoms and bring you back on course with another question or by prompting you.

Crib notes
It's always worth taking notes into a radio interview. If your mind does go blank you can always refer to your notes and carry on. But don't prepare a full script because the temptation is to read it word-for-word, which will rob the interview of all its spontaneity. The only time you can get away with reading a script is if you are giving the media a pre-prepared statement on an issue where exact wording is important for legal or other reasons. Lawyers frequently read pre-prepared statements on behalf of their client, for example.

Even brief crib notes don't usually work on television. Every interviewer's nightmare is the interviewee who lays out shoals of notes on the table as a sort of security blanket. If you keep looking down at your notes you will appear unprepared and lacking in authority. The only way to ensure you don't lose your thread during a television interview is to memorise your key points and try to hold them in your mind's eye as you speak. An exception is if your argument includes figures. These are easy to get wrong, so a brief note in front of you *is* permissible. In that particular instance the odd glance down for reference won't look awkward, but don't overdo it.

What comeback do I have?
What do you do if, despite your best efforts, you are unhappy with the broadcast version of your interview, or the reporter has acted with little regard for people or property?

If it's a matter of interpretation then bite your tongue. The reporter is not your PR consultant and s/he may have a preferred idea of your story, whatever your best efforts to persuade him or her to your viewpoint. If the reporter's view is valid and the facts accurate you can't really complain and you won't get much joy if you do. Equally, if you say something in the interview which you later have cause to regret when the interview is transmitted you can't blame the reporter for using the material you gave – unless it was clearly understood that the comment was off the record.

If there's an obvious and serious factual error then phone the newsroom and point the problem out immediately. Sound bites from your interview may be repeated several times in successive bulletins, and extended interviews may be repeated at least once in the course of a local radio breakfast show. If you don't point out the error it will go out again and again. Most radio and television stations will be grateful for your call and amend the story before it is transmitted again.

If you feel you have been libelled, or your privacy invaded, or you have a complaint about the behaviour of a reporter, call the station and ask to speak to the editor or manager. Inevitably, his or her first concern will be to protect the reporter concerned, but if your complaint is genuine and serious you can expect the editor to take action.

If you don't receive satisfaction from the station's management, contact the Broadcasting Complaints Commission. Its role is to adjudicate independently on complaints against broadcasters.

8

HOW TO PROJECT AN EFFECTIVE IMAGE

There is frequent criticism of the media for its obsession with image. The fear is that the way we look and sound has become more important than what we say and that we are becoming a culture of 'cardboard cut-outs'.

Image *is* important in the media because it's all the audience knows about us. We are divorced from the listener or viewer not just by distance, but time too. When we appear on television we aren't really sitting in people's living rooms; when we take part in a radio interview we may be many miles away from the listener's transistor set. If the interview was pre-recorded it may be transmitted hours or even days after we actually spoke into the microphone. When we appear on radio or television our appearance is an illusion, a flickering of electrons across a screen or inside a speaker, which the brain of the viewer or listener interprets as evidence of our reality. As the audience cannot know us as real, living, breathing people whose actions and thoughts they can judge for themselves, we have to concentrate on making sure the image we present through the media goes as far as possible towards making us 'three dimensional' to bridge that gap between illusion and reality.

When handling newspaper interviews *what* you say is all-important. With radio, *how you say* what you say is important. In television, *how you look* while you say what you're saying has a vital impact on the way the viewers view you and your message. If you look confident and authoritative, the audience will believe you and trust what you're saying. If you look hesitant and shifty and stumble your way through your answers, the audience will write you off in seconds.

Psychologists say we make up our minds about people less than a minute after meeting them. That impression is created by the way we dress, the way we speak and through our body language.

A fashion guide for interviews

No-one expects you to carry round a wardrobe of special clothes on the off-chance you may be interviewed by a television crew. You should feel as natural as possible when you meet the film crew or turn up in the studio, but there are some ''do's'' and ''don'ts'' which will help you look your best.

Generally, sober colours and simple patterns work best on television. Unless there is a good reason for you to look casual, dress smartly. Remember, you will be appearing in people's homes.

- Avoid wearing too much *white,* it can make you look fatter than you really are and also dazzle the television camera's 'electronic eye'. A white shirt or blouse half hidden by a jacket is OK.
- Too much *black* can make you look severe. Also, the camera can have difficulty picking out the detail so your head and hands will appear to be separated by large areas of impenetrable shadow.
- Three colours to be wary of are *bright red, mid blue and green*. The camera finds it difficult to cope with bright scarlet, so your tie or scarf will glow so brightly you appear to have a bonfire on your chest! The reason for not wearing mid-blue or certain shades of mid-green in studio interviews is a technical one. These are the colours used for a special technique called *Colour Separation Overlay*, or CSO. This device is used to project background images onto the screen. The weather map that the weather presenters refer to isn't really behind them. The presenter is actually waving at a blank blue or green screen, onto which the weather map is projected as the programme is transmitted. If you were to wander in front of the camera wearing a blue or green top the weather map would be projected onto your torso! If blue and green are your colours don't avoid them altogether, but do check with the producer first whether it's all right to wear them.

- Give 'busy' patterns a miss. Thin stripes or small checks on a shirt, blouse or suit can confuse the camera's electronics, causing an effect the technical people call 'strobing'. On screen you'll appear to have thin coloured 'worms' crawling over you, or your clothing will appear to buzz and vibrate under the camera lights.

- If you customarily wear a particular sort of garment, don't change for the interview. What you wear helps identify you to the audience: businessmen wear suits, scientists wear white lab coats and surgeons wear surgical gowns and so on. To illustrate how important clothing can be to your image, imagine a surgeon being interviewed wearing a chef's hat. The viewer would be deeply confused as to what the interview was all about!

- Sometimes informality or a deliberate change in dress may work in your favour. If you want to appear relaxed and informal and the setting is appropriate, wear whatever suits the occasion and the image you want to convey. For instance, if you are a spokesman for a pesticide manufacturer and you are promoting a new 'green' herbicide you wouldn't want to be interviewed in a pin stripe suit or even a white lab coat. To emphasise the user-friendly nature of the product you would opt to wear casual gardening clothes in a garden location.

- If you are required to wear safety equipment such as goggles or a hard hat in the course of your work, use them in the interview. It will set a good example to the watching public and avoid awkward questions from the Health and Safety Executive.

If you are preparing for a radio interview, clearly what you look like is immaterial. There is no point in you turning up for an interview in a suit and tie if you are not used to formal wear. Dress for comfort. You will perform much better if you feel relaxed.

Accessories
Avoid wearing an intricate brooch or tie with complex patterns. The viewer may spend much of your interview trying to work out the design rather than listening to what you're saying.

If you normally wear a name badge, take it off – it will distract the viewer's attention from what you say. During the interview the camera may be on a wide angle setting, showing your head and upper body and a good deal of the background behind you. At that range the viewers will see you have a badge on but they won't be able to read it, and they may well spend much of the interview trying to decipher the writing on the badge rather than listening to what you say. The reporter will ensure your name and organisation are shown by means of a caption thrown up on the screen when your interview goes out.

If you're being interviewed outside in the sun, or under bright studio lights, be wary of sunglasses or Reactolite spectacles. We rely heavily on eye contact to gauge people's sincerity and if the audience can't see your eyes they may distrust you and your message. If you rely heavily on your spectacles and would look odd or owlish without them point out the problem to the reporter or the cameraman and suggest you're interviewed in the shade where the glasses will clear and allow the viewer to see your eyes.

In a radio interview, beware of accessories which create noise. Cufflinks make an irritating ticking noise if you move your wrists around on a hard desk top, and change or key 'janglers' need to empty their pockets before entering the studio.

It need hardly be added that in both television and radio interviews loud interruptions are the last thing you want. If you have to wear that modern ball and chain, the message pager or bleep – or you customarily have a mobile phone close to hand – do make sure it is turned off for the duration of the interview. And remember to turn it back on again afterwards!

Make-up
Make-up is not usually required if you're being filmed outdoors; the camera will record your colouring faithfully in natural sunlight. If it's very hot and you perspire a lot, a light dusting powder may be necessary to help keep your face or forehead from shining.

Artificial lights, such as those found in a studio, will not be so kind to you; you may acquire a rather alarming grey or even green pallor. Professional television presenters almost always wear make-up to restore a healthy colour to their face. You may be offered make-up for that reason. If you don't normally wear make-up and wouldn't have a clue how to apply it, assistance is usually at hand. If you need help, ask for it in good time.

Make the most of your voice

The way you speak is important to putting your message across in an interview. In radio the listeners can't see you, so all they have is your voice. In television the viewer can see you as well as hear you, but how you sound is still important. No-one expects you to be a voice-over artist and it's important that you remain yourself, but you can help yourself by making the most of your voice.

Suit the tone of voice to the subject

If it's a happy topic or something you're enthusiastic about, sound happy or enthusiastic; the audience won't be enthused if your delivery is deadpan and downbeat. If the subject is a serious one and you're seeking to reassure the public, try to sound concerned yet calm and authoritative.

The 'bedside manner'

If you're in a hole and your only escape is to brazen it out try to sound convincing and reassuring, however you might feel inside. You're being interviewed because your role in the story is significant, so the way the public perceives the issue will be coloured by the attitude and image you project. The so-called 'doctor's bedside manner' is an excellent example of how this works. The last thing the patient wants is for the doctor to admit it's not clear what's wrong and that the prognosis is disturbing. A good doctor hides such concerns and by tone of voice reassures the patient that all is under control and the problem will be sorted out successfully. A convincing, confident tone of voice will help hide any amount of real uncertainty in what you say.

If you're talking on behalf of an organisation and you're required to deliver a 'party line' with which you privately disagree, be careful this cynicism doesn't appear in your voice. The audience will spot your insincerity and your credibility will be lost. Don't complicate matters by trying to draw out subtle differences between the 'party line' and your own view. There will be no time to put such nuances across in a two or three minute interview.

Speak clearly and don't rush

Many people naturally talk fast, especially if they feel stressed. This is fine up to a point. However, if you speak *too* fast the viewer or listener may not catch all you say, and you may also say things you regret. By pacing yourself you will give the audience a better chance to follow what you're saying, there's less chance you will say something you don't mean and any pauses will be dramatic rather than a panicky hesitation. News readers are taught to speak at around three words a second. This is probably a little too slow for a normal interview, but speaking slower rather than faster does minimise the chance of a stumble and will allow you to put emphasis into what you say.

Don't worry over much about the occasional 'err' or 'um'. The odd audible hesitation is natural, but too many can be painfully obvious and distract the viewer or listener from what you're saying. If you feel you have a problem the cause may be one of two things: you may be speaking too fast, which forces you to stop while you think what to say next, or you may not have prepared your facts for the interview. Pace your delivery, it will help your brain keep up with your tongue so any pauses will be conscious and deliberate. If you prepare properly for the interview you will be clear in your mind what you want to say and how you wish to respond to predictable questions so you shouldn't have to hesitate while you seek inspiration.

Body language

As with clothes and image, what your body language says doesn't matter on radio, but it does matter on television. Be aware of any mannerisms which may betray the way you're thinking, or, worse, inadvertently give the wrong impression. If you're trying to persuade the audience that your argument is convincing and believable, licking your lips nervously at the wrong point can give the contrary impression.

Don't slouch – it'll make you look sloppy and indifferent. If you're seated, sit up straight so you appear relaxed but alert. Don't overdo it though. Appearing to have a broom handle up the back of your shirt or dress can make you look wooden and stiff. If you're standing for the interview, adopt an upright posture without leaning to one side or another.

Be aware of your expression. Some people adopt a forced smile or grimace under stress; if you are talking about something

serious a smile of any sort would give the wrong impression.
However, do try to put some animation into your expression; a
little mobility in the face can go a long way towards making you
seem confident and relaxed, even if that's not the way you feel
inside!

Eye contact
Make bold eye contact with the interviewer. It's an excellent way
to appear sincere and in control. This may not come naturally.
We normally only look directly at people for any length of time if
we're being intense. Direct eye contact implies desire, anger or
some other strong emotion. In casual conversation we normally
look away frequently to signal our relaxed mood; we may drop
direct eye contact completely to indicate to the listener that we
don't mean what we're saying at that point in the conversation, or
perhaps to signify boredom with the other person's point of view.
On television this impression comes across very strongly. Looking away implies indifference or shiftiness – so be wary. If you
want to convince the audience that you mean what you say or that
you're in control of an awkward situation then let your eyes do
the talking.

Under the stress of an interview people often demonstrate
strange foibles which they don't realise at the time.

Some people look up at the ceiling for inspiration. A quick
glance upwards is natural. It can signify momentary impatience,
which might be appropriate and quite effective if faced with a
point of view or question with which you strongly disagree. But
gaze at the ceiling or sky for any length of time and you will
appear pompous and superior.

Other people tend to look at their feet. In real life we hang our
heads in shame if we know we've done wrong. Doing the same
on television will transmit exactly the same impression to the
audience. If you're trying to convince the viewer that you're
totally in command of the situation breaking eye contact down-
wards will give entirely the wrong idea.

Some people break eye contact left and right, particularly if an
aggressive interviewer is pursuing an assertive line of questioning. Faced with aggression we instinctively look away to avoid
further antagonising the other person. The trouble is, if you do
this on television you will appear shifty and uncertain and may
well appear to be seeking a means of escape. This, of course,

may be the way you *feel*, but you don't want the viewer (or the reporter) to know that.

Finally, some people shut their eyes so they can concentrate while they talk. This can look very odd on television. If the viewers can't see your eyes they don't know what you're thinking. The subconscious impression will be that you're hiding something.

Be sensible

If you're to think quickly and put your arguments across clearly in a broadcast interview it's important that you feel on top form. The evidence of a late evening out may be only too visible in the bags under your eyes. Try to get a good night's sleep before an early morning interview.

Never be tempted to a try a little Dutch courage before taking part in a broadcast. Alcohol may make you feel more relaxed, but in fact it blunts your reactions and may noticeably slur your speech. Even a half pint of beer or a small glass of wine may affect your performance as a number of broadcast journalists, including the author, have found to their cost!

Leave yourself plenty of time to get to the interview. The last thing you want is to arrive rushed and bad tempered – it won't do anything for your state of mind, or the calm and assured image you wish to present. Estimate how much time you will need to get to the studio in good time, then double it. Traffic, parking problems and trying to find the studio can all take more time than you bargain for.

Practise and review

Practise before the interview. Ask a friend or close colleague to put you through your paces, and watch out for problems with your body language. You may not even realise you have strange mannerisms until they're pointed out to you.

Some stress 'tics' don't show themselves until you experience the pressure of a real, or seemingly real, interview situation. A good way to work on your presentation under more realistic conditions is through media training (see Chapter 12).

After the interview, try to obtain a video or audio recording of your performance. You are most unlikely to persuade the radio or television station to provide this for you, at least not for free, as it takes up valuable staff time. The simple and easy answer is to arrange for someone to record the interview for you on a domestic video recorder or radio tape deck. Of course, if your interview was pre-recorded you will be able to see or hear yourself when the interview is transmitted.

Listen and watch closely, and avoid the temptation to cringe at every mistake – they're sure to have been less obvious to the audience. Decide what faults, if any, are serious enough to merit rectifying and resolve to do better next time!

9

THE RADIO EXPERIENCE

Radio is an excellent medium to use if you want your message to reach a wide range of people quickly and reliably. A local radio interview will be listened to by the same audience that reads the local papers. The same interview on a major national network will be heard by members of Government and other power brokers, as well as millions of ordinary folk. That makes radio a powerful and influential publicity tool. It's fast too. Radio is technically simple, so, if necessary, a story can be turned round in minutes. Unlike a newspaper interview which is subject to the whims of the reporter, what you say on radio is, more or less, what goes out to the public so there's less chance the facts and the quotes in your story will be altered or abused. Unlike a television interview, you don't need to worry about how you look, just how you sound.

The studio interview
If you are interviewed live, the chances are the interview will take place in one of a number of self-contained studios at the radio station. Large stations will have several; smaller stations will have just two.

   The radio studio often doubles up as a technical control room, especially in local radio. The programme presenter operates all the equipment as well as talking to the audience and carrying out interviews. In front of the presenter is a large control desk, covered in switches, slider controls and dials; to each side are the various machines needed to produce the programme, record and CD decks, tape machines, telephone mixers to control phone-in programmes and a number of microphones. In some studios much of the technical business is now handled by computer. The walls are coated in thick soundproofing, while heavy doors prevent the intrusion of stray sound from outside. This unfamiliar environment can be unnerving the first time you step into the studio. If you find the opportunity, a trip round your local radio station before you do your interview can be helpful, if only to give you an idea of what you will face.

The type of programmes presented depends on the radio station, its style and its target audience. You may be asked to take part in one of the following.

The magazine show

This, despite the name, is not about glossy publications. The programme imitates the mixed content of a magazine. A typical show might comprise news, weather, traffic updates, and interviews or packages covering a huge range of topics. It's a format used widely for breakfast shows and their end-of-day equivalent, the 'drive time' programme. Programmes like this have a voracious appetite for interviews. One local radio breakfast show alone may well feature over twenty interviews a week. Yours could be one of them.

You'll be asked to take part in a magazine show if your topic is of interest in itself, or because the programme wants your reaction or comment on a topical story. The programme makers may come to you, or you may have generated the interest yourself by sending a press release to the programme producer. Either way the first contact will be a phone call from the producer or perhaps a researcher. This will usually be the day before but the call may come just hours before the show goes out. Take this opportunity to find out what the interview's about (see Chapter 7 'How To Handle A Broadcast Interview'). Brief the producer or researcher on the story and what you'll say. If the interview is to be live it's important to have your discussion at this stage as you won't have another opportunity. When you meet the presenter it will be in the studio and you'll have little or no time for chat. The presenter will be working from a *cue*, a briefing sheet and list of suggested questions provided by the producer. So if you fail to brief the producer properly, don't be surprised if the interview doesn't go as smoothly as you'd like.

Arrive in good time for the interview. You won't give of your best if you're flustered and out of breath. If the interview is very early in the morning or late at night you may have to find a back

door if reception is shut. Ring the entry phone, identify yourself
and someone will let you in. If it's not offered, do ask for a
coffee, tea, or glass of water if you want one.

Ask how the interviewer will introduce you. If you don't
correct any mistakes or inaccuracies now you may not get a
chance later.

Shortly before the allotted time for the interview you will be
shown through to the studio and given a seat opposite one of a
number of microphones. Don't speak until you're spoken to as
the presenter may well be talking 'on air' as you're ushered
quietly in. As soon as s/he gets a chance, perhaps while a tape or
disc is playing, the presenter will greet you, adjust your microphone and perform a quick 'level check' on your voice. This is
usually done by asking you what you had for breakfast. Speak in
your normal tone of voice and don't lean towards the microphone. In fact, ignore the microphone altogether. After reading
the cue, or introduction, the presenter will launch straight into the
interview.

Most magazine shows work on a series of two to three minute
time slots. If you're well prepared you can cram a lot of
information into three minutes; if you're not prepared the interview will be over before you know it. Be clear in your mind what
you want to say and make sure you say it.

Don't be surprised if at some stage of the interview the
presenter turns away from you and fiddles with something
technical. S/he isn't being rude. The presenter has a lot to do as
well as talking to you, so ignore the interruption and keep talking.
On balance, it's an advantage to you because while the presenter
isn't paying attention to what you're saying s/he can't pick up on
any flaws in your argument!

After the interview you will be ushered rapidly out of the
studio. You may well not have an opportunity to speak to the
presenter and without the pat on the back you feel you deserve
you can feel abandoned and 'used'. Don't assume you've per-
formed poorly, it's just that a live show has a lot of momentum
and rarely is there time for feedback or a gentle 'wind down'.

Chat shows
Many radio programmes have at least an element of extended
discussion. They pick a subject, possibly a topic which is currently in the news, and examine the issues in more depth than

would be possible in a news or magazine programme. The discussion is likely to be more wide ranging and there'll be more time. Chat show conversations vary between five and sixty minutes in length. You may be on your own with the presenter or there may be other guests with different perspectives from yours.

The advantage of the chat show is that it gives you a lot of air time to voice your opinions or state your case, but you do need to prepare well before-hand. The longer the interview, the more facts you're going to need at your fingertips.

Phone-ins

This is a popular form of programme because phone-ins are cheap to produce and offer a high degree of listener participation. You, and perhaps others, will be asked to come into the studio and talk about an issue. The presenter will then open the phone lines for the public to call in and either express views or ask questions. If your topic is controversial you can be sure the programme producer will have found a number of other guests whose views are diametrically opposite to yours; a good argument makes for better radio! On the other hand, if yours is a specialist subject which doesn't have any clear element of controversy you may be alone with the presenter.

Phone-ins can be a good source of free publicity. You'll often get a lot of time – perhaps as much as an hour – to talk about your subject. Also, you'll be talking directly to the public which gives you an opportunity to inform and educate or influence the audience.

Talking directly to the public may, however, pose a considerable challenge to your tact and tolerance as only the most obviously manic callers will be filtered out before they are put on air. Some stations, but by no means all, operate a 'bleep' system to guard against callers swearing or libelling anyone on air; the programme is fed through a delay system which allows a few seconds for offending comments to be erased. On other stations the filtering is done by an assistant who takes the calls and puts them through to the studio.

Anticipate a mixed bag of callers. Some will be well informed on your subject and if they are opposed to your position may well give you a worse roasting than the most aggressive journalist. Others will be looking for advice, or simply to express an opinion.

As with most things, preparation is the secret to handling a
phone-in. Think through all the issues which are likely to crop up
and work out how you'll respond. Never get angry or aggressive,
however the caller behaves; and don't patronise, no matter how
foolish the question or point of view put forward. You will
achieve far more by pursuing a line of polite but firm, reasoned
argument.

Take a pad of paper and pen with you into the studio. Make a
note of the caller's name and use it during your discussion, it will
make you sound human and approachable. If you're stumped for
an answer to a question, promise to find out the relevant information and report back to the programme or the caller concerned.
And do make sure you carry out your promise otherwise you will
wreck your credibility with that caller at least, and possibly other
listeners.

The 'down the line' studio interview
It may not always be possible for you to travel to a radio station's
main studio for an interview. Radio stations can cover a large
area, especially in rural districts. Many stations therefore have
small studios dotted around their 'patch' to enable them to
interview guests in broadcast quality from outlying areas. From
the 'sub-studio' you will be interviewed 'down the line' by a
presenter or reporter at the main studio.

Local radio stations have their own sub-studios based in
council offices or police stations, or some other centre. National
networks will have smaller studios dedicated to their own use at
provincial centres, often in local radio stations. The development
of a new breed of digital telephone link, called ISDN lines,
allows the transmission of broadcast quality sound over long
distance. Many larger authorities and concerns whose staff have
regular contact with the media have taken advantage of this new
technology to set up small sub-studios in their own buildings.
This means staff can give interviews without having to leave their
place of work.

Sub-studios are often small – little more than a room or a
cubicle which has been roughly soundproofed. The equipment
will be simple, consisting of a microphone, telephone, headphones and a small control desk. Rarely will there be anyone to
operate the equipment for you, though suitably qualified staff
may be available to help if the sub-studio is in a radio station.

Otherwise you're on your own and you'll have to establish contact with the mother studio yourself. There is usually a comprehensive list of instructions to guide you. Generally, this is a straightforward and logical procedure, "Sit down at desk . . . phone the following number to establish contact . . . press red button to switch on microphone . . ." and so on.

Some people are more technically proficient than others. You may have to put your thinking cap on before mastering the equipment, so arrive with plenty of time to spare before the interview is scheduled to take place. You will not give of your best in the interview if you arrive ten minutes before the recording or transmission and then panic because you can't understand the studio instructions. If in doubt, concentrate on phoning the studio on the telephone. Once you've established contact someone technically qualified will talk you through the rest of the connection procedure from the other end.

When the studios are linked to everyone's satisfaction you will be put through to the presenter or reporter who will interview you, though sometimes it will be the programme's producer who will speak to you first. You should not expect to go 'on air' straight away. There should be time for a very brief preliminary chat, during which time you can ask any last minute questions you may still have about the programme and your contribution. If it's a live interview you will hear the programme through your headphones. If the presenter needs to talk to you at this time s/he will override the programme to do so. Don't worry that what you say at this point will go out on air, though never risk a dangerously unguarded comment! You will know when you are finally on air, because the presenter will announce you and launch into the interview.

If your contribution is being recorded, the procedure is similar to a live interview, but a little simpler. The reporter or presenter will chat to you, then proceed directly to the interview.

If you are unused to broadcasting you may find it unnerving talking on your own in a small studio. In fact, until you are a competent broadcaster with several interviews under your belt, you may prefer to be interviewed in the main studio, even if it means travelling some distance. The main problem with the sub-studio interview is that the interviewer isn't there with you. You have no visual contact, so you have no idea how what you're saying is being received, or when to stop and let the interviewer talk. In normal conversation we rely heavily on body language to give us important clues as to the other person's reactions to what we say. That's missing in the sub-studio situation. The answer is simple. Focus on what you want to say, say it, then stop – and wait for the next question. Many people are afraid of 'dead air' and talk too much. Don't worry. If you stop, the interviewer will butt in with another question. It's better to be concise than chatter away and lose your thread . . . and possibly the listener.

If there is a technical problem during the interview, or you can't hear clearly, say so. 'Soldiering on regardless' may be helpful to the broadcasters but it will give the wrong impression to the listeners, who may not realise your hesitations or apparent random deviations are caused by a technical fault.

Once the interview is over you will hear the interviewer thank you and then move on to another topic if the show is live. Do wait a second unless you're in a hurry. As soon as s/he can the presenter will return to you 'off air' and thank you for your contribution. Take the headphones off and leave the studio, turning off the power if requested to do so.

The telephone interview
Improvements in the technical quality of telephone lines means that many radio stations will choose to carry out what's called a 'phono' in the trade. Very often telephone interviews are carried out when speed is of the essence; the reporter may be looking for a brief quote, or sound bite, of 20 to 40 seconds duration, rather than a full interview. If this is what the reporter asks for, compose your response accordingly.

From your point of view, the telephone interview is straightforward. You don't need to go anywhere, you're on 'home ground' and you're familiar with the instrument. But the telephone interview can be dangerous. The very familiarity of the technique may mean you drop your guard, forgetting that your casual chat with the presenter or reporter will be played to thousands of people. Be on your mettle. One way to sharpen your wits is to stand up during the interview. Because you wouldn't normally chat on the phone while standing to attention you make yourself aware that this is not a normal telephone call and that you should be careful what you say.

The telephone interview should be in two parts, the brief

preliminary chat, which is 'off air', and the actual interview which will be transmitted or recorded.

The preliminary chat is often done with the reporter talking to you from a conventional phone in the newsroom. To record the interview s/he will then hurry through to a studio and you will be asked to hang on while the call is transferred. Don't be surprised if the line goes dead, junior reporters in particular have a capacity for pressing the wrong buttons in the studio and losing the call. Put the phone down and wait for them to call you back. Once your call is 'through the desk', in other words transferred into the recording equipment, the reporter will ask you to identify yourself on tape and then commence the interview.

If the interview is live, the presenter will briefly chat to you then put you on 'hold', but in such a way that you can hear the programme going out. You will hear yourself being introduced and then the first question, which is your cue to start talking.

As with all other interviews, insist on your right to know what's going on before you do the interview. Ask which station you're talking to, what the subject is, whether the interview will be recorded or 'live', and so on. Don't be bullied into an instant response and if you feel you need a little time to prepare ask the station to call you back a little later. Some stations will try and catch you off guard by putting you straight on air the minute you answer the phone. If this happens to you don't slam the phone down, it will only make matters worse and imply you have something to hide. Try to do the best you can, but telephone the station afterwards and complain to the radio station manager.

Secret recordings

BBC reporters are required to tell you clearly when they are recording what you say and when they're not. Other news organisations may not have the same restriction. If in doubt, ask. Above all, never say anything near a microphone or camera which could cause damage if it is recorded or transmitted.

Noises off

When you're doing a telephone interview resist the temptation to have the programme playing on a radio in the background so you can hear it, or so your family can admire your performance. If the telephone can pick up your voice on the radio it will create a horrible shrieking feedback effect. If the radio is on quietly in another room the problem won't arise.

Mobile phones
It is unlikely that the radio station will agree to an interview by mobile phone, except in an emergency. The signal on most mobile phones is very poor and by the time it comes out of the tinny speaker of the listener's transistor radio your interview will be unintelligible.

The 'simul rec', or simultaneous recording
This is a variation on the pre-recorded telephone interview which allows your interview to be transmitted in broadcast quality even though the reporter may not be able to get to you, or you to the studio. It's not a widely used technique but it's worth knowing what will happen. The reporter (or presenter) who wants to interview you will despatch a colleague from a nearby radio station to your home or office with a portable tape recorder. The presenter will then phone you and ask questions which s/he records in the studio. You will hear the questions over the phone, and the person who's with you records your answers on tape. The answers are then passed to the presenter who knits the recorded questions and answers together so it appears you were together in the studio for the whole interview.

The location interview
In radio, sound is everything. It's the audio equivalent of the picture in the newspaper. In other words, it can say much about the interviewee and the story which couldn't be provided by speech alone. If your story offers the possibility of interesting background sounds then the radio reporter will want to come to you. Alternatively, the reporter may need to come and see you because you can't get to the studio. This type of interview, recorded 'on site', is called a 'location' interview.

The pre-recorded location interview
Recording a radio location interview is very straightforward. The reporter will turn up with a tape recorder and microphone. Many BBC local radio stations still use Uher tape recorders – large and heavy machines the size of a large satchel which record onto old fashioned ¼″ tape contained on open 5″ spools. Though cumbersome, the Uher's solid build and ability to withstand knocks has

Sound is everything in radio.

made it the industry standard for many years. Commercial radio
stations and network BBC programmes prefer to use professional
quality cassette recorders. These are smaller and lighter to carry,
offer very acceptable quality and allow long recordings to be
made. Many stations now use disc recorders which fit in the palm
of the hand and give extremely high quality. The microphones
used with all tape and disc recorders are hand held and attached to
the recorder by a length of cable (the microphones built into many
tape recorders don't offer adequate quality for broadcasting).

The location interview may be recorded anywhere: at your
office or home, or in your factory, or in the countryside if that
setting is appropriate. The reporter will opt for your home or
office if the main focus is what you say and no sound effects are
to be had, or indeed are relevant. If, on the other hand, background sounds are important to your story, the reporter will want
to record the interview where the sounds are. For instance, if the
subject is steam engines the reporter would want to carry out the

interview in the engine shed or on the foot plate of a locomotive.

Suitable background noises will make the report sound much better. If the story is about wild geese, clearly all the punch of the interview will be lost if it's recorded in the quiet ambience of an office. It should be recorded with geese honking audibly in the background.

"Does it make a noise?" will often be one of the first questions the radio station puts to you when you're first contacted. If the answer's yes, then agree to an on-site interview. If the station doesn't ask, mention the possibilities yourself, either over the phone on first contact or when the reporter arrives for the interview.

Once on site, be patient while the reporter seeks out the best place for the interview. S/he may well have to balance the sound of your voice and the background sound, or you may have to wait for a suitable sound (animals in particular have a tendency to go quiet just when you don't want them to). At the other extreme, some sounds intrude when they're least wanted. Noisy jet aircraft can appear without warning, even in the most rural areas, and you may have to abort the interview until the interruption has stopped.

Sometimes the reporter will want to record sound separately, rather than as a background to your interview. This 'wildtrack' sound is useful if your interview is to be included in a 'package' (see Chapter 7). The sounds may be mixed under your interview, or they may be used as a background to the reporter's script to make it appear the script was read on site.

Some large news organisations have extensive sound effects libraries and these can be used to provide suitable material for use in a package, but the reporter will still try and record sound on site if possible. Very often the most comprehensive sound archive won't have exactly the right sound needed for a piece and if the wrong sound is used, well-informed members of the public are not hesitant in pointing out the error. It's amazing how many people know what sort of sound a particular bird should make at particular times of the year!

If you are to be interviewed in your office or home, there's a lot you can do to ensure the interview runs smoothly. Assuming you have established before-hand that the reporter wants to carry out this type of interview, choose a room with reasonable acoustics. You don't have to be a sound engineer for this. Choose a room without high ceilings and with a reasonable degree of soft furnishing – curtains, carpet and so on – to help absorb sound. Stand in the middle of the room and clap your hands. Is there a noticeable boom or echo to the sound? If so, find an alternative location. An interview recorded in a big, sparsely furnished room will not improve the quality of the message you are trying to put across. If your place of work is an open plan office, beg the use of a colleague's enclosed room, even it means pleading with your boss; explain that the background chatter of others will distract the listener's attention from the interview itself.

Deflect interruptions. Murphy's Law will ensure that at the climax of the interview your phone will ring or a colleague will stick their head round the door with a query. If this happens you may never recover, so prevent it happening. Take the phone off the hook or have your calls diverted so the phone doesn't ring. Hang a 'Do Not Disturb' notice on the door or ask someone to field any visitors. If the interview is in your home, persuade the kids to keep quiet or go somewhere else, and, again, take the phone off the hook.

When the reporter turns up don't try to intimidate him or her by insisting s/he sits the other side of your desk or living room table. This can be very tempting if you feel a deep-seated desire to keep the 'enemy' at arm's length, but there are good reasons not to do so. First, wide flat desk tops can adversely affect the quality of the recording by bouncing the sound of your voice around. Secondly, nearly all radio interviews are conducted using hand held microphones which don't have long cables, aren't mounted on an extendible boom and work best if held around 40cm from the interviewee's mouth. You and the interviewer will have to be close enough together to allow the reporter to hold the microphone near you without arm strain. The most comfortable position for this type of interview is side by side on a settee, or, if you are in the office, arrange two chairs at a corner of your desk so you and the reporter are in close proximity.

This set up may be unsettling at first. The optimum distance between you and the reporter may well fall within your 'personal space' so you will feel uncomfortable; we normally only invade each other's space if we are threatening or flirting. To add to the strain, the microphone looks like a balled fist or stick and the reporter, a stranger, is asking you assertive or even aggressive questions. The result can be a potent and primitive cocktail of emotions – not least of which is a strong desire to lash out or lose your temper!

There are things you can do to diffuse the situation. First, remember most radio interviews are informational and won't involve a head on confrontation. Secondly, if you sit at an angle to the reporter rather than face to face, the body language you unconsciously associate with threat will be toned down. Thirdly, you can always give your interview standing up. This will seem more natural and allow you to feel more on equal terms with the interviewer, especially if you are taller.

After a preliminary chat, the reporter will want to set your recording level. Older tape machines need to be adjusted manually to the strength of your voice, so be patient – this check only takes a few seconds. Usually the reporter will ask you some innocuous question such as "What did you have for your breakfast?" and monitor the level of your answer. Don't give a one word reply. Invent a cholesterol rich diet to give the reporter time to set your level properly. Try to talk naturally. It won't help matters if you whisper during the level check and then talk much louder in the interview, or vice versa. And don't be tempted to be witty or say anything you may regret if it's ever transmitted.

The next step may be a request for your name and title. Some reporters will launch straight into the interview after recording your personal details in a notebook. Others will prefer to have your identity recorded on tape before the interview so they don't mix you up with somebody else.

Once the interview starts, concentrate on what you're saying. Ignore the microphone. Don't lean towards it, or even look at it. The reporter will move the microphone if s/he needs to. Simply look the reporter in the eye and focus on giving simple, concise answers to the questions asked.

After the interview, the reporter will want to play back a short section of the recording to make sure it's OK. Be prepared to do the interview again if there is a problem.

Don't ask to hear the interview all the way through afterwards, unless the subject is highly sensitive. Minor glitches will stick out like sore thumbs and you may well want to record the whole thing again. The glitches are not usually as serious as you think and second attempts at interviews are rarely as good as the first. But, if you've made a real hash of an answer, by all means point this out to the reporter and s/he should let you attempt that answer, or the whole interview, again. After all, it's in the reporter's interests for your interview to be polished and accurate, if only because it will reflect well on them!

When everything is finished, the reporter will bid you farewell, pack up the equipment and depart. Be sure not to let your guard drop with the relief of completing the interview. No reputable reporter will attempt to record what you say without you knowing, but his or her eyes and ears won't be switched off at the same time as the tape recorder. Any confidences you impart as the reporter is at the door may find themselves in the report even though what you say hasn't actually been recorded on tape.

The radio car interview
You may be interviewed live, or pre-recorded, from a radio car. The radio car is effectively a mobile studio contained in a conventional car or van modified to contain a radio transmitter and extendible aerial. Some radio cars are big enough to allow interviews to be conducted inside. The BBC in London, for instance, uses a converted 'black cab'. Other radio cars are smaller and packed with technical equipment, so your interview will need to be carried out standing next to the car, or, via extension leads, in a nearby building.

Radio cars offer stations the chance to go anywhere in the station's area and are frequently used to transmit reports and eye witness accounts from the scenes of accidents or other sudden events. They can also be used to report on outdoor events, like fêtes, or air shows. Whole programmes are sometimes produced in this way, with the presenter 'anchoring' the show from the event, while discs and taped interviews are played in from the main studios.

You may be interviewed either by the person with the radio car, or by a presenter in the studio. In the latter case, you will hear his or her questions through headphones. Do ask before-hand which scenario you are likely to face.

10

THE TELEVISION EXPERIENCE

Television interviews offer a greater opportunity to put your message across to the public than their radio equivalents. They're also a bigger challenge. There's the added visual element, so you have to think not just about *what* you say and *how* you say it, but also how you *look* while you say it.

Television can be fun, bringing out the actor in some people. It is also a powerful communication medium, so if you get the chance to put your message across on television, seize the opportunity with both hands.

To make the most of a television interview it's important that you're thoroughly prepared, not only for likely questions and the arguments you want to put to the audience but also for the unfamiliarity of the television interview in all its different flavours.

As with radio, there are two types of interview in television: the studio interview and the location interview. Either may be *live* or *pre-recorded*.

Live interviews can be nerve wracking, at least before-hand. This is because you will know you only have one chance to get it right and there's no chance of stopping to correct a mistake. There's a feeling of performance, that you will be meeting your audience head on. On the other hand, the live interview does have its advantages, the most significant being that what you say goes out unaltered and there's no chance of a journalist being able to cut bits out of your interview. So if you get the chance and you want your argument to be transmitted in its full form, opt for the live interview.

By definition, a pre-recorded interview takes place some time before it is transmitted. The interview may be going out just a few hours later. This is common if you are interviewed for a news or magazine programme which is transmitted later that day. On the other hand, your interview could be kept for weeks before being used. This may happen if you are interviewed for a documentary. Documentaries are complex programmes which may involve weeks of research and the recording of dozens of interviews. In some rare cases it may be months before your interview sees the light of day.

Pre-recorded interviews are generally less stressful. If you (or the reporter) fluffs or makes a mistake, you can always stop and start again. The problem from your point of view is that the pre-recorded interview is not always transmitted full length. Only a portion of the interview may be shown; bits may be cut out to make it flow better or to fit the time span that's been allotted to the story. If getting your whole message out on air is important to you and you have the choice, opt for the live interview.

The live studio interview

Leave plenty of time to get to the television studio. If you don't want to be flustered by traffic, take a taxi, or the studio may offer to collect you. Large television companies have many different departments so be clear which programme you have been asked to appear on and who to ask for on arrival.

You will nearly always have the chance to chat with the presenter and any fellow guests before the interview. Most stations have a hospitality suite, called the *green room*, set aside for this purpose. If you are offered alcohol, refuse. Even a small tot may take the edge off your performance. Steer clear of sweetened tea or coffee because they will clog the palate, and sparkling mineral water because the bubbles may repeat just when you don't want them to. Unless you're starving to the point where hunger may affect your performance don't eat immediately before the interview. Your mouth will continue to salivate long after you've licked the last crumb from your lips, which can do strange things to your speech.

The pre-interview chat with the presenter and/or producer is a chance for you to pin down exactly which direction the interview will take; feel free to ask about anything which concerns or puzzles you. It's also an opportunity for you to set your own ground rules. If there's an aspect of the story you are not prepared to comment upon, now is the time to make that clear. However, be aware that this invites the interviewer to put that very question to you in the hope that you *will* talk on the subject once the interview is in full flow!

Don't let nerves trick you into revealing more than you should, share confidences, or throw yourself on the mercy of the presenter. Points you make in the preliminary chat may come back at you in the interview.

If you've done your home work you will already know who, if anyone, will be appearing with you. If it's someone with an opposing viewpoint don't be tempted to argue your case at this stage – save the fireworks for the interview itself.

After the green room you may be taken to make-up. Make-up will help you look healthy and natural under the glare of the artificial studio lights. Accept gracefully whatever powders and lotions are deemed necessary to silence the glow from your bald pate or shiny forehead.

Studios can be intimidating places. High ceilings, huge curtains, complicated cameras and batteries of bright lights can all conspire to make you feel nervous and uncertain. Try to concentrate on why you're there and the arguments you want to put over. Your mouth may suddenly go dry. If water hasn't been provided, feel free to ask for it. If necessary, follow the advice given on page 80 to try and calm any butterflies.

In the studio with you will be the presenter and any other guests. There may also be several technicians loping noiselessly around in the shadows, though increasingly studio cameras are operated by remote control. All the television staff will be able to communicate with each other and the director in the *gallery* (control room) through what's called 'talk back' – small throat microphones and ear pieces. You won't have this luxury, which can make you feel isolated and unloved. Look on this as an advantage as at least you will be left in peace to think without distraction. If the director needs to say anything to you s/he will communicate through the *floor manager,* whose job is to make sure everything in the studio runs smoothly. Be wary of microphones; just because you can't hear what other people are saying don't assume what you say can't be heard.

Once the run up to the interview has started, look at the presenter. The cameras will probably be on you before it's your turn to speak so don't choose this moment to pick your nose or make faces. Avoid the temptation to look round or up at the lights, you may become disorientated and certainly half blinded. Concentrate on what you want to say, recall your main points and launch into your answers.

After the interview, look steadily at the presenter – you may still be 'in shot' and unguarded expressions or gesticulations may detract from the authority of your interview. Don't assume the interview is over until you are physically 'rescued' and ushered out of the studio.

The 'as-live' studio interview
The 'studio as-live' is a pre-recorded interview but it's carried out in all respects as if it *is* live. Live interviews always contain an element of risk; interviewees can fail to turn up, dry up on air and take longer or shorter than expected to make their points. The cautious producer may opt to pre-record the interview so its quality can be checked and, if necessary, shortened to fit the available time slot for its transmission. The producer will want the audience to think the interview is live so the interviewer will wear the same clothes and make-up s/he will wear when presenting the programme. The back drop will also be the same as that used during the programme. In short, there should be no clues to the audience that the interview isn't being played out as it happens. You'll know of course, because you were there, and you may be comfortably curled up at home watching the television as your 'live' interview goes out.

Because the 'as-live' interview is supposed to be exactly that, if you 'fluff' an answer you should try to keep going. But if you have made a serious factual error, or if you lose your way completely, don't be afraid to call a halt and ask if you can start the interview again.

The 'down the line', or remote, studio interview
Most television stations cover large areas. Many stations therefore have a number of small remote studios in various locations so no interviewee should have to travel very far to reach a studio. These studios are usually very small, often little more than a cubicle or small room, perhaps rented from a local council or based at a local radio station. They are generally equipped with a single camera, a bank of lights, a microphone, a chair and perhaps a table but very little else.

There is rarely a member of staff at the studio to conduct

interviews. You'll be interviewed by a reporter or presenter in the main studios which may be many miles away. You'll hear the questions through a small ear piece or perhaps a speaker and address your answers to the camera. The resulting interview is either recorded the other end for later transmission or transmitted live.

You will be shown into the studio by someone who knows how to switch the equipment on, apply your make-up if necessary, fit your ear piece and ensure you are comfortable. Ask for water if it hasn't been provided.

The first voice you will hear will be that of the presenter or reporter who is interviewing you, or possibly the director who co-ordinates the technical side of the interview. If there's time, ask any final questions you may have about the interview and the area of questioning.

The director will decide where you should look. Many stations require you to look straight at the camera. This will create the impression that you are talking directly to the viewer. Peering into the lens itself can make you appear to have a slight squint, so you could be asked to talk at a point just above the lens. Many cameras have a small red light which shows they're operating. This can be a good focus for the eyes.

Depending on the station style, you may be asked to look away from the camera and towards some arbitrary focal point in the studio. This is to make it seem as if you are looking at the presenter if you both appear on the same screen in the final transmission. Don't be thrown if you are asked to address your argument to the handle of a coffee cup or a fly speck on the wall!

As with radio, the most intimidating thing about a television 'down the line' studio interview is the lack of eye contact with the interviewer. In everyday conversation we rely heavily on facial body language to assess our listener's reaction, to judge their interest, understanding or their intention to interject with another question. In a remote studio you have none of that. The sense of unreality can be made worse by the strangeness of your surroundings. You may feel as if you're talking to yourself in a goldfish bowl of light. The only way to handle such an interview effectively is to be very clear about what you want to say, say it, then stop. The interviewer will then fire another question at you. Try and relax if you can. Allow some animation into your face and voice. Under stress it's very easy to look and sound like a

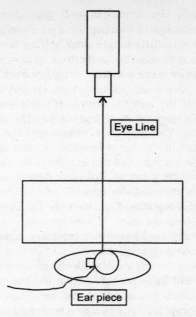

Eye Line

Ear piece

Fig. 1 The down the line TV studio interview (top view)

robot. Maintain eye contact with the lens and avoid the temptation to glance sideways when the interviewer is speaking into
your ear piece.

Remember, the camera may be on you immediately before and
immediately after the interview, so don't relax, pull faces, or
make unguarded comments when you think you're 'off air'. You
will destroy the credibility of the interview you have just given or
are about to give.

The location interview

A 'location' is what radio and television people call anywhere
away from the studio. It may be in your office, your home or out
in the countryside. The location interview is usually pre-recorded,
though there is an exception we will come to later.

Television interviews generally take longer than a radio interview and you will want to be certain you can allow enough time
to do a thorough job without rushing yourself or the television

crew. How long the interview will take depends on several factors. If the station is looking for a straightforward quote the interview may take little longer than half an hour, but if you are the subject of a documentary or the topic is complex and there's a lot to film you can wave goodbye to half or even most of the day.

How many people are going to turn up and walk mud across your carpets? If the story is simple it's not uncommon for the camera person to turn up alone and ask you the questions after the camera is set up. You may also come across the *video journalist*. As broadcast quality cameras become smaller and easier to use, some television stations are cutting costs by issuing journalists with cameras so they can record their own material. A regional television news crew usually consists of two people: the camera operator and the reporter. Occasionally the camera person may also bring a sound operator. If your interview is to be part of a documentary there could also be a producer, a director, a production assistant and a lighting expert.

You may have to wait a while for the reporter and film crew to turn up. Both will have probably been working on another story before they come to you and they may have had quite a long way to travel. You can use this waiting time to prepare your arguments and think through what you want to say. Don't be surprised if the crew turns up before the reporter, or vice versa. Reporters and camera crews rarely travel together. Once a reporter has finished a story, s/he can race back to the studio to process the material while the camera crew can be sent off to cover another story, either alone or with another reporter.

When the crew arrives, offer tea or coffee and other hospitable pleasantries. Being nice can pay dividends. The crew may have travelled a long way to reach you and a timely cup of tea, even a sandwich, is likely to improve their frame of mind and possibly their attitude to you and your point of view. If parking is at a premium near your home or office try to make two car parking spaces available, preferably close to where the interview will take place. Camera equipment is heavy and the camera operator will not thank you if s/he has to lug a camera, lights and tripod half a mile to reach the interview site.

Be sure to have a chat with the reporter before the interview. S/he may have very little idea of what the story is about and it's in your interest to brief him or her on the subject of the interview. Don't bore the reporter with reams of detail, but do satisfy

Some TV stations expect the journalist to do everything.

yourself that s/he has a reasonable idea of the basics. Don't say
anything you wouldn't want broadcast or which might be thrown
back at you in the interview. Remember, the interview doesn't
start and end with the camera being switched on and off. The
reporter's memory can be a potent recording tool.

The backdrop
After a quick chat with you the crew will want to look round for the
best spot for the interview. The backdrop to an interview is very
important to its success. It can provide a good deal of information
about you; if you are an academic you will be interviewed with
books in the background; if you're a chef the reporter will want you
standing in your kitchen, and so on. Generally speaking, the crew
will not try to make a fool of you by choosing an inappropriate
backdrop. It's different if you're a politician in the public eye.
Camera operators have a lot of fun at election time trying to
persuade cabinet ministers to stand in front of escalator signs saying

'Down', or sale signs announcing 'Only three days to go'. That's unlikely to happen to you, but don't be too complacent.

Check whether the crew's ideas accord with what you know to be wise, especially if the story or the work you do is sensitive and controversial. For instance, if you're the manager of a poultry farm and the reporter wants to interview you in front of penned battery fowl you might decide the negative impression given to the public by that particular shot outweighs the benefits of doing the interview. If you have strong feelings about the inappropriate nature of the backdrop to the interview don't be afraid to say so and suggest an alternative you feel would be better for your image.

Once the backdrop to the interview is agreed the camera operator will set up the camera tripod and a portable light if the interview is to take place indoors. You may be asked to stand, or the interview may be conducted with both you and the interviewer seated. If you are interviewed standing up and you are substantially taller or shorter than the interviewer then one of you may have to stand on something to bring your 'eye lines' level.

Just before the interview begins the camera person will need to adjust the equipment for the level for your voice. You will be asked some innocuous question such as what you had for breakfast. Don't just mutter 'toast', speak for long enough to allow the sound level adjustment to be made.

At this stage, the camera operator may also ask the reporter for a 'white', at which point the reporter will hold up a notebook or other white object in front of your face. This is to allow the camera to be adjusted to the prevailing lighting. Our eyes adjust automatically to different conditions, but a camera has to be told the lighting has changed. If the adjustment isn't made your skin may undergo a colour change which is anything but flattering!

Ask the camera person or reporter if your appearance needs fine tuning. Your hair may be mussed, or if you wear a neck tie the knot may have slipped. Trust the advice you receive; no-one will try to make you look silly.

Once the interview starts, look at the interviewer, not the camera. Location interviews appear odd if the viewer knows the interviewer is there and the interviewee is addressing the camera directly. This is actually an advantage to you as it's much easier to hold a conversation with a real person than with the camera lens.

The reporter will wait until the camera operator advises it's

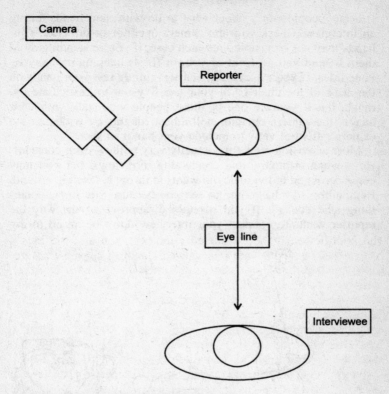

Fig 2. The location TV interview (top view)

OK to start and the reporter will then launch into the first question. Maintain strong eye contact with the interviewer throughout the interview and try to look relaxed. Resist any temptation to rock backwards and forwards on your heels as you will drift in and out of focus. If you're seated during the interview don't swing nervously from side to side as the camera person will have to move the camera to follow you. This will cause the background to appear to move rhythmically behind you, which can make the audience feel seasick!

If you want to refer to something during the interview, don't turn to point to it or say "as you can see behind me". Additional shots of the subject can be filmed later and interleaved with your interview back in the studio.

Some people worry about what to do with their hands during an interview. Check with the camera operator or director. Your hands may not be visible, in which case, if you're standing, hold them behind you, in front of you, or (best) hanging casually by your sides. If you're seated it's easier: simply rest your hands on the arms of the chair or in your lap. Try not to gesticulate too much, but if you are one of those people who 'talk with their hands' the camera operator will adjust for this by widening the camera's field of view to include your hands in shot.

Most television crews are actually very polite – even considerate – when arranging and conducting interviews, but you may come across an individual who wants to throw his weight around. Remember, s/he has come to see you because you know something s/he doesn't. If you strongly disapprove of the way the reporter wants to conduct your interview don't be afraid to dig

If you disapprove of the way the camera crew wants to portray you, say so.

your heels in. It's important that the interview works for you as well as the television station, so stand up for yourself. Having said that, don't be obstinate if you have no real grounds for objection. The television crew knows more about how to conduct effective interviews than you do, so unless you are sure they're against you or have a hidden agenda, assume that what's being done will make the programme and you look your best.

Set up shots
Once the interview is over, the camera crew will want to film whatever it is you've been talking about. This can take more time than you might anticipate. Just a couple of minutes of well shot and professionally produced television can take an hour or more to film. The camera person will want to get a variety of shots which can mean repeating an operation several times. Put up with this gracefully because a well shot item will show you and your message to best advantage.

Even if you have only been asked for a quote the crew will still want shots they can use to introduce you. It would look odd if you suddenly appear in the programme with no introduction. If you are a major player in the piece the camera crew will ask you to act a little so as to give them shots they can use to show while describing who you are and what you do. If you are a model engineer they would want shots of you working on a model, or at a lathe; the chef will need to be seen testing a dish; the cabinet minister will be depicted signing important papers. If you are a gardener or work outdoors you will be asked for a 'walking' shot; either on your own or with the reporter you will be required to walk past the camera, pausing occasionally to poke a plant or examine something.

If you feel the set up shots the crew have asked for are banal or make you look self-conscious or ridiculous, say so. Suggest instead that you do something more original and relevant to the subject of the interview. Journalists and camera operators resort to clichéd shots simply because they haven't thought of a good alternative.

Other set up shots called 'cutaways' may be recorded to allow the reporter to cover any edits s/he may want to make to the interview afterwards. If a section of a television piece is cut out, the edit is very visible – buses suddenly disappear and interviewees' heads jump magically from one part of the screen to another, for example. To disguise these cuts other shots are interleaved with the interview at the edit point. This may be a rear view of

you and the interviewer talking (called a 'two shot') or it may be
a 'noddy' (a close up of you or the interviewer nodding atten-
tively as if listening to an interesting question or answer). Editing
is not usually done to distort your message; it may be necessary
to cut the interview in length or to remove time-wasting hesitations, repetitions and deviations.

If there is only one camera on location, as is usual, it will have
been focused on you. What are called 'reverse shots' may
therefore be taken of the interviewer repeating questions asked in
the interview. The reporter may want to repeat questions without
you present. Be wary, it's possible the repeated question may be
stronger than the original, or the reporter may want to change the
wording so as to put a different slant on your answer. If you're
worried make sure you hang around to hear the new version.

Some reporters will suggest phrases for you to use and even try
to coax you into putting your arguments in a certain way. This
could well be to your benefit. S/he may see a clearer way for you
to put your argument. This will nearly always be the case but
don't be too trusting. S/he may be working towards an ill-
conceived (from your point of view) stereotype of your story. If
the journalist's suggestion seems to make sense, go along with it.
If it doesn't, say so – and stick to your guns!

The outside broadcast interview
The Outside Broadcast location interview (or OB) is an increasingly popular format. Thanks to improvements in technology it's
now easy to transmit interviews over great distances using satellites
or a microwave link, which means that television stations can now
do live interviews on location. The technology comes in the form of
a large van with a dish aerial or mast with an antenna on top.
Because it's mobile the van can be driven anywhere.

Producers like to use live location interviews because they
make the station's coverage seem more immediate and local to
viewers. The exact format of the broadcast depends on the story.
If your event has plenty of colour and potentially· interesting
interviewees it may be used as the focus for a whole programme.
The programme's presenter will turn up in person and present the
whole show from your event, interleaving live commentary on
what's going on with pre-recorded items on other issues which
are played out from the studio.

If it's a serious news story the format will be different. As the story breaks, the producer will send a reporter and camera crew to the scene to pick up early pictures and report on the action as it happens. These first pictures will be sent back to the studio to be made into a 'package'. This pre-recorded report will be played out during the programme, and then the presenter will 'return' to the scene of the incident for an update from the reporter, and possibly an interview with a key character or spokesman in the drama.

If you are asked to make an appearance during an outside broadcast expect the following.

The presenter will 'hand over' to the reporter. The reporter then briefly introduces the story or sets the scene with a short 'piece to camera', then turns to you to ask you questions. At all times keep your eyes on the interviewer and don't be tempted to look at the camera – it has a 'Hi Mom!' quality (see figure 3).

Expect the unexpected in a live OB interview. If the producer is short of time, it's possible the interview will be only one question and answer long. That means you have very little time to make the points you want to make. For this reason if you are doing a live outside broadcast interview it's important that you bring out your main point straight away. Don't wait for an opportunity to slip your message in later, because you may never

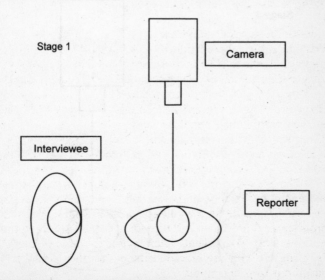

Fig. 3 The outside broadcast location interview (3 stages)

Stage 2

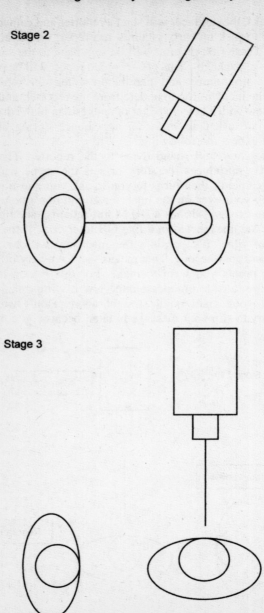

Stage 3

get the chance. At the other extreme, the producer of the programme may find s/he has more time than expected, perhaps because the next item in the programme has been delayed, so the reporter will be asked to extend the interview until the producer is happy to move on. In this case you may find the reporter asks you a series of questions which become more and more desperate as s/he tries to fill time. Look on this extended interview as a bonus. The more air time you are granted, the more opportunity you have to bring out all the positive things you have to say about the situation.

11

HOW TO MANAGE
A CRISIS

Publicity is a double edged sword. It's a powerful and cost effective way of reaching a large public, which is fine if you want to promote a policy, product, or event or persuade the public to your point of view. But if your policy is controversial, your event has caused trouble, or something has gone badly wrong, the media may come knocking on your door just when you *don't* want publicity.

Bad news travels fast. When something goes wrong the media swing into action at bewildering speed. You may have a bevy of reporters on your doorstep before you even know you have a crisis. The press pack is only the tip of the iceberg. Relatives of workers, shareholders, local leaders and the general public will want to know what's going on and they'll want to know quickly. If the crisis involves a chemical incident, nuclear alert or serious pollution, uncertainty will be exacerbated by fear, and the public's need for information may be compounded by hysteria.

A really big news story that has international dimensions can be a huge drain on an organisation's resources. Little Dumfries and Galloway, the smallest of Scotland's police forces, could not have coped alone in the aftermath of the Lockerbie air disaster in December 1988. The media very quickly outnumbered residents and it took 160 press officers to deal with all the enquiries which followed for many weeks afterwards. Spokespeople found themselves talking by satellite to all corners of the globe at all hours of the day and night.

While no one can predict when a crisis will strike, there are several things you can do to minimise the damage.

A stitch in time . . .

A drama only becomes a crisis if you don't or can't control it. Preparation is the key to handling negative publicity; anticipating the worst so that when it does happen a crisis management plan slips smoothly and efficiently into action.

The first step to preparing a crisis management plan is to be ruthlessly critical of your organisation. Don't be taken in by your own PR. No corporate strategy is perfect; no industrial process is failure-proof. Machines break down, humans err and the result can be catastrophic. Bargain on the worst happening and plan accordingly. If you view your operations through rose tinted spectacles you will be caught on the hop when something goes wrong. It may be a good idea to commission an independent consultant to give you an impartial and independent view of the strengths and weaknesses of your operation (see 'media audit' page 139).

Lay the ground for trust before-hand

If you try and create a positive public image during a crisis it's too late. The time to build up trust and public confidence is before the incident. A rock solid corporate image created through years of constant communication with your neighbours, local authorities and the media will pay dividends when things go wrong. Concern over the incident itself will be tempered by familiarity with, and trust in, your organisation.

Some well intentioned PR moves may backfire. One chemical company which produced a range of hazardous substances had a sign by its main gate which spelt out the number of days since the last accident on the site. Its purpose was to impress the workforce with the need to be safety conscious. Unfortunately the sign also re-enforced the public view that the site was prone to accident by highlighting every new incident. It was a natural subject for television pictures should a serious incident occur.

Appoint a crisis management team

It doesn't fall within the remit of this book to explore every aspect of crisis control, but having a clearly defined team to establish and oversee precautionary plans is well advised. This should not be an *ad hoc* team which meets only when there *is* a crisis. The team should be a permanent one, with regular meetings at which plans can be formulated and updated. Large industries maintain teams on permanent standby so they can be reached quickly in an emergency.

It's important that all key managers are party to crisis management planning and this should clearly include the PR manager as well as operational heads. In a crisis PR is not a bolt-on luxury, it is an essential to maintaining the organisation's corporate image so that, whatever else ensues from the crisis, unnecessary bad publicity is not the main by-product.

Select a suitable spokesperson

Choose a suitable spokesperson in advance. This may not necessarily be the most senior line manager in charge of handling the incident; s/he will be too busy dealing with the crisis itself. Nor is it necessarily the senior press officer. The media will want to speak to a company representative who is clearly involved at the cutting edge of handling the crisis itself. Key interviews should be handled by a senior management figure. When the Bhopal disaster struck, Warren Anderson, the chief executive of Union Carbide, handed over the day-to-day running of the company so that he could personally manage the crisis. As a result Union Carbide had a 'face', a personality. This arguably demonstrated that the multi-national was concerned, and showed it could not only shoulder the blame but was also prepared to mobilise its resources to solve the problem.

It's important the spokesperson should be a capable and experienced communicator. The wrong person flung into the limelight at a time of crisis may wreck all your hard work and behind-the-scenes organisation, simply through poor presentation. Choose someone senior enough to have authority, but who can be freed from the minute-to-minute handling of the emergency. That person should have considerable experience of handling the media. S/he should be able to remain calm under intense pressure and have the natural ability to *appear* confident, concerned and reassuring even when all is crumbling around them.

It is vital the spokesperson knows the limits of what s/he can and can't say. It is very easy to be 'sandbagged' by knowledgeable journalists and forced into saying something inappropriate. One of the biggest difficulties is knowing when to say "no" to reporters without appearing to get into an argument. One way is to identify the key points that need to be put across and then use a form of 'mantra' which can be repeated, in different ways if necessary, without departing from the core set of points you have drawn up.

Address problem issues early
If you delegate media contact to staff involved in an area of operations which may have a negative public image, be sure those staff know how to deal with media enquiries about the issues and the appropriate responses to give to specific predictable questions.

If necessary, convene a meeting between the staff concerned and PR advisors to thrash out what the central issues are, the potential pitfalls and possible ways to put a positive spin on negative aspects of the subject which may emerge in an interview.

Maintain contact lists
Identify which branches of the media will be most likely to cover a given crisis. If the incident is serious enough this is likely to be almost every major news organisation in the country. A minor problem will be covered by the local and regional media in depth, but you may escape the attentions of the national press and broadcast channels. Draw up lists of newsroom telephone and fax numbers, e-mail addresses and editors' names, and *keep those lists updated*. Note that most newsroom numbers are ex-directory so you may have difficulty finding them in a crisis; keep up-to-date lists of contact numbers to hand at all times.

Prepare to brief the media
Initially most reporters covering the crisis will know little of your operation, so they may have difficulty reporting the incident accurately. Take the initiative in advance by preparing briefing packs which explain what you do and spell out your procedures for handling a crisis. Prompt distribution of briefing material to journalists immediately the crisis happens will demonstrate your commitment to communicating with the public. It will also encourage the journalists to focus on your interpretation of events and the efforts you are making to control the incident.

When preparing your briefing be aware that opposition groups which may criticise your position are increasingly cunning in their manipulation of public fears and prejudices. You should not rely simply on the often impenetrable language of science when faced with a campaign from a pressure group that targets the fears of a scientifically unsophisticated public. The oil giant Shell discovered this to its cost when Greenpeace forced the company to abandon plans to sink its Brent Spar rig in the ocean. Although Shell could line up ranks of experts to prove it was right in terms of waste disposal options, Greenpeace used psychology rather than science to create a consumer boycott which in turn forced a Government and company climbdown.

Plan a media centre

Don't assume you can control the media from your headquarters if it's miles from the incident. Have contingency plans to set up temporary media centres close to every potential crisis site. This will give a point of focus for the journalists and allow you to corral them in one place. Warm journalists with access to a coffee machine are less likely to wander off in search of eye witnesses you'd rather they didn't meet if they are getting reliable information and frequent updates from you. But reporters will only submit to your control if you give them what they want. Don't regard the media centre as a temporary 'lock up' – the journalists will soon escape, with disastrous consequences for you. Provide them with regular updates on what's happening, allow them to check their stories with you or someone in authority (but don't insist on it as that will put their backs up) and make arrangements for regular, controlled photo or filming opportunities.

It is better to 'manage' film crews and photographers by setting up facilities which give them action shots than risk them running amok. During the Strangeways prison riots in Manchester the media was denied access to the prison itself. Undeterred, the photographers simply took vantage points in neighbouring tower blocks and filmed everything they could see. By comparison, photographers at the scene of the Clapham rail crash were quickly directed to a nearby bridge where they were able to film – at a tasteful distance – scenes that told the story words could not.

When preparing a media centre, scout out suitable locations, such as hotels, or village halls, before-hand. Make plans for the rapid installation of telephones, faxes and modem terminals. The rapid growth in the availability of palmtop computers with built in cellphone modems means that in future there may be less need to lay on conventional communication facilities.

Set up an emergency communications room

Not all journalists will actually turn up at the control centre; many will phone in for quotes and updates. Ensure you have a suitably equipped communications centre close to the emergency control room so updates on the situation can be quickly passed to the media. This will need to be staffed by suitably trained and briefed PR personnel. Arrangements should be made so that key personnel can be brought to the communications room quickly. It should not be forgotten that it may be necessary to transport them some distance if the control room is far from their normal place of work.

In a crisis it can be difficult extracting information from emergency controllers who are handling the incident itself. If effective communications are to be maintained it's important the senior public relations manager has unquestioned access to the control room and is known to the controllers.

If possible the emergency communications centre should be equipped with a 'quiet room' where press releases can be prepared away from the distracting hubbub of the communications room. If the number of press office staff available is limited, draft in suitably briefed people to answer phones so the press officers can concentrate on preparing press releases which inform and reassure. Answerphones will only frustrate and anger those who consider they have a right to immediate answers. Consider arranging a freephone recorded 'update' line for those unable to get through to the main switchboard.

Brief your staff

The value of an accurate, concise question and answer brief can't be overstated. As soon as a 'crisis situation' has been declared a brief should be drawn up (with assistance from the highest levels) and distributed to all those who could find themselves answering questions from the media or other external audiences. Take steps to ensure this briefing is kept confidential – there is no point in revealing to the media details of the situation they have not asked about!

Ensure everyone knows the proper channels

In a crisis it's vital that everyone pulls in the same direction; the most carefully laid plans can go wrong if key personnel don't know how to route information.

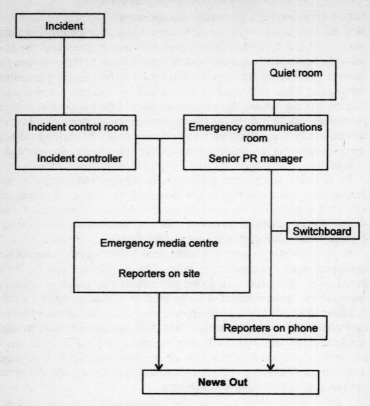

Fig. 4 Lines of communication in a crisis

The humble switchboard operator has an important role in a crisis, yet is often overlooked. In the mid-1980s news reached the BBC local radio station in Essex that a helicopter had been hijacked from an airport 'somewhere in England' to assist the escape of a prisoner from a high security prison. At that time I had responsibility for covering Stansted Airport in Essex, so my news editor asked me to check if the helicopter came from there. I put in a speculative call to one of the two helicopter hire firms then working from the airport. Immediately I identified myself as a reporter to the switchboard operator she replied that she was unable to tell the press anything about the hijack and put the phone down. That one remark immediately put the firm in the centre of the media spotlight. Doubtless, the company had been told by the police not to speak to the media for fear of making the situation worse. The point is, no-one would have known the identity of the firm concerned for some hours if the switchboard operator had been properly briefed on how she should respond to media calls.

Ensure that your switchboard staff have clear guidelines as to what they should do in an emergency. They should have immediate access to a list of relevant emergency numbers and should put all media calls through to the appropriate people. They should not volunteer information under any circumstances.

Ensure you have direct lines to any other organisation that could be implicated and maintain constant contact throughout the crisis. Consistency of message is crucial. Some years ago there were severe floods at the Welsh town of Tywyn. Spokesmen from different authorities ended up blaming each other on screen – they clearly hadn't talked to each other before going on camera.

The media conference
Media, or "press", conferences are of limited use when announcing day to day news or launching a new product, but the conference comes into its own in a crisis.

Holding a media conference gives you the chance to update reporters without having to repeat your message for different journalists. It also provides a central focus from which to project a cohesive and positive image and associated messages of concern, regret and action taken.

Be prepared
Preparation is vital for the successful crisis media conference. If you appear confused or ill-informed the media will detect this straight away. Have the facts at your fingertips and be as transparent with the truth as possible. If there are aspects to the crisis you want to keep quiet, be careful. Journalists may discover from some other source that you're trying to hide something and if they do your credibility will evaporate like snow in summer.

Be seen to be in control
If your press conference is well organised and the spokesperson puts across relevant information in a crisp and informative

manner, this is the impression the journalists will convey in their reports.

Pick the time of your main press conference carefully. Be aware of reporters' deadlines. Leave your press conference too late and you may miss key bulletins or newspaper editions. Twelve noon will give time for your quotes to find their way into both the evening papers and the lunchtime and evening television bulletins. You can always issue further updates through smaller-scale briefings later in the day; in fact this can be a useful ploy, as it will give you the last word and may pre-empt attempts by journalists to obtain contradictory statements from other sources. Even if a television or radio journalist has filed his or her main report, late breaking news can usually be included in the bulletin along the lines of "We've just heard that . . .", so long as the new information doesn't mean the whole report has to be re-written.

Set a time limit for the press conference. Give yourself enough room to say all you have to say and field a range of questions, but don't leave yourself in the firing line for too long as this can be dangerous. You may run out of things to talk about, and frustrate journalists who are itching to get away to file their reports. Around half an hour is probably about right. Make this time limit clear at the start of the conference.

Outline the background to the crisis. Use this opportunity to re-emphasise positive points in your favour but admit fault where this is unavoidable and don't try to hide glaring errors. If relevant, use visual aids such as maps, models or diagrams to explain important details but don't attempt complex presentations which are more suited to a sales conference – you may appear unconcerned with the grim realities of the incident.

Keep it simple, and human

Keep your delivery direct, simple and unadorned. Use ordinary English and don't stray into jargon which will leave journalists struggling to understand a complicated situation. In particular, don't use official terms which may make you seem distant and uncaring. For instance, if you're trying to reassure people after a river has burst its banks, using the word 'flood' will win you more respect from your waterlogged audience than the more bureaucratic 'flooding event'. To those who heard and watched military press conferences during the Gulf War phrases such as 'collateral damage' and the unbeatable 'rotational hexiform fastening device' (for which read 'nut') may have been amusing, but such terms did not bring home the impact of military operations. Such euphemisms have their place in time of war as they help to temper the emotional impact of cruel realities on a sensitive public. If you're trying to put a human face on an accidental disaster, everyday language people can understand will serve you best.

Issue accurate updates

Once you have finished explaining the background to the situation give the latest information you have to hand. The more information you volunteer, the less likely journalists are to question your position. Stress the efforts you are making to contain or control the crisis and highlight everything positive you can find to say. If expressions of regret are appropriate make them convincingly and sincerely, don't beat your breast in dismay, and move on quickly to make positive points about your efforts to control and limit the damage.

If you give out information to one journalist you should give it to all. Each journalist will be seeking a 'scoop' to boost his or her reputation and s/he will be delighted if you single him or her out for special attention. But short-changing one news organisation to benefit another will not help you at all. The recipient of the 'scoop' is unlikely to be any kinder to you as a result, *and* you'll have made enemies of other members of the 'media pack'.

Taking questions

Once you have outlined the latest situation, allow questions. Ask each journalist to identify themselves as this will give you a few seconds to marshal your thoughts. It will also give you some indication of their approach and the way your answer will be treated. Anticipate likely issues that will be raised and have suitable answers ready. If you can't answer a question, don't waffle; give a sensible reason as to why you can't address that point and promise a response as soon as you have one.

Don't be bullied into saying anything you don't want to. Also, don't be drawn into speculating on the cause of the incident unless it is absolutely clear cut. If you do speculate on the cause and you're subsequently proved wrong – in particular if you have imputed blame to an organisation or individual which is later proved innocent – you will appear at best incompetent, and you may risk being sued for libel by the injured party. Faced with the question "What went wrong?", or "Witnesses say it was . . ." simply reply that it's too early to speculate and that everything possible is being done to establish the cause.

Be assertive and don't let the question and answer session go on too long. After giving the journalists a good run for their money, signal your intention to end the session by offering to take just one more question and then stick to that decision. When leaving the press conference do so decisively, but don't rush – it will make it appear as if you are trying to escape and the cameras will still be rolling and the microphones recording. If you are unfamiliar with the geography of the conference centre don't fall into the same trap as the new college tutor who, at the close of his maiden lecture, strode from the podium and through the nearest door – only to find himself in a broom cupboard. He eventually sheepishly re-emerged to find his students patiently waiting for him to come out!

Make sure you know what is being said about you
Any crisis PR plan must include arrangements to record the radio and television news bulletins which could be carrying the story. It is vital that you are aware of what is being said so you can tailor your PR strategy accordingly. If the media has got the wrong end of the stick, or is not concentrating on the real issue, you can then do something about it. If there is a glaring error you should call the station concerned immediately so the offending interpretation can be corrected in future bulletins or editions. There are commercial monitoring companies which will carry out this task for you.

Monitoring the media has a dual purpose – it assists at the time to ensure you deliver the right messages and it also enables you afterwards to assess your organisation's performance in a crisis and learn lessons for next time.

Crises and the individual
Crises don't just happen to large organisations, they can happen to individuals too. So, what do you do if you suddenly find yourself in the limelight when the last thing you want or need is intense media interest?

Do you want to talk to the media?
Ask yourself if there is anything to be gained from agreeing to
media interviews. Give the idea serious consideration; there may
be assumptions and misconceptions you need to dispel which the
media will run unchecked if you don't intervene. Even though the
charges against you (whatever they are) may not be true, refusing
to comment always carries the implication that you are guilty as
charged.

You can run, but you can't hide!
Lying low for a while might seem like a good idea, but you
should realise that if the story is good enough journalists have
the tenacity and the financial backing to find you anywhere. It
may therefore be in your interest to make at least a brief
appearance to diffuse media attention. While not wishing to
push the analogy too far, the media operate in something like a
hunting pack, with you as the quarry. If you run, the journalists' instinct is to pursue. If you turn and face your tormentors
they may back off, especially as they're not after your blood
but pictures and a good quote. Give both and the chances are
the 'press pack' will slink away into the shadows whence they
came.

Choose the right place and moment for your media appearance.
You may have noticed that MPs accused of sexual impropriety
pick suitably domestic settings for their impromptu press conferences, and will (if they can) appear with the allegedly hard-
done-by spouse and family close at hand. If you are responding to
accusations of 'fat cat' salary awards meeting the press as you
step from your Rolls Royce in full view of your swimming pool
may not create the impression of injured innocence you would
ideally want to convey.

As to what you should say if you do give an interview, stick to
the following guidelines:

- try to appear calm
- give the background as you see it
- express regret (if necessary) and sound sincere, but don't
  overdo it
- be positive
- spell out any action you may be taking to put the damage
  right.

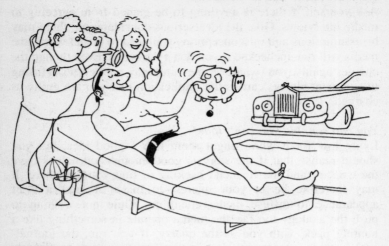

The wrong setting can conflict with your message.

Handling the 'door step' interview

If an important story develops quickly journalists won't take the time to telephone you to arrange an interview. They'll turn up on your doorstep, unannounced, and you may emerge from a meeting or your living room to find a sea of journalists waiting expectantly for a quote. This can be very intimidating and the natural tendency is to run for cover. But offering no comment can be damaging, so if you can, steel yourself to meet the rat pack. Take heart – if you handle a 'door step' interview the right way you may well win sympathy from viewers or listeners. Unless you are very clearly the 'black hat' in the situation, and provided you give a good account of yourself, the audience will probably side with you.

Be aware of how you look and sound

Stay calm, or least try to! In this sort of situation how you appear will determine how the public views your position. Body language is everything. If you look shifty and avoid eye contact with journalists, the public will assume you are guilty or have something to hide, regardless of what you say.

Take the initiative
The journalists will all want to get a quote from you. This can lead to an atmosphere of chaotic competition as each reporter pleads for a comment. You can expect a clamour of voices all demanding a quote, and questions will be fired at you from all directions. It's up to you to impose a little order on the situation.

Let the journalists know that you're willing to be interviewed. This will immediately take some heat out of the situation as they realise a free-for-all isn't necessary to get a response from you.

Insist on taking questions one at a time. This will force the journalists to effectively queue for their turn with you. Because they realise they have a good chance of getting their question in they will usually accede to your request for calm. They will wait their turn and listen to other questions and the answers you give.

Ask each journalist to identify themselves. This has two advantages for you. Firstly, your assertiveness will help to impose further control over the throng. Secondly, you will get an idea of who's who, and knowing who you're talking to will allow you to tailor your answers accordingly. For instance, you may want to give a more fulsome response to the representative of a national broadsheet than the local radio station.

Be positive. If things have gone wrong, stress any remedial steps you have taken to put things right. If the public needs reassurance then give that reassurance.

Be aware that while newspaper reporters can use answers you give to other journalists, television and radio reporters will prefer to record their own interviews. If you feel you have the time and the inclination then offer individual interviews.

The door step interview is very intimidating and stressful. The emphasis is on you to make the best of the situation. But don't leave yourself exposed for too long – you may be caught by a question you'd rather not face. Give the journalists enough to feed on and then retire gracefully, promising a later update if that is appropriate.

12

TAKING IT FURTHER

You should by now have a clear idea of how to handle publicity to your benefit; how to seek it, how to manipulate it, and how to cope with bad publicity. Where do you go from here? If after having read this book you have appreciated the potential benefits of handling publicity the right way you may want to look at developing a long term publicity and PR strategy.

Many smaller organisations don't have the luxury of a department to handle marketing or press issues. Nonetheless, there's a lot you can do to establish a PR strategy yourself.

The PR agency
One way round the expense of running a full time PR department is to engage the services of a public relations agency. Good PR agencies can provide excellent value for money. They will liaise between you and the media, advise on how to publicise specific products or policies, and draft and send out press releases to appropriate news outlets. But do be careful. A small minority of firms capitalise on the client's ignorance of the media. They may take little interest in servicing your account effectively and simply send off press releases on a 'blanket' basis whenever they see fit. This is a waste of your money, so choose an agency which can demonstrate it has your interests at heart.

Going it alone
There is no reason why you should not assume control of your own PR affairs, especially if your concern is small. If you follow the guidelines in this book you will have the knowledge, and the experience will come with time.

Assessing what you've got

Just as every business or operation has a financial worth, it also has a value in publicity terms. Different aspects of the operation may be potentially newsworthy, either in a positive or negative sense. To run a successful PR strategy you need to know the potential newsworthiness of your operation and where the areas of strength and weakness are.

If you are new to the publicity game you may be too close to your operation to assess this objectively. You might therefore want to consider commissioning a *media audit*. This involves bringing in a professional PR consultant to assess each aspect of your operation for its news potential.

Choose a PR consultancy with a strong journalistic bent. A successful media audit requires the skills of an experienced reporter to assess potential stories. The difference is that this journalist will report what s/he finds to *you* rather than the public at large!

Media training

Handling media interviews is a practical skill. A good guide will give you the necessary *knowledge* but learning to handle interviews effectively is a bit like riding a bike. No book can help you with that first wobbly expedition down the front drive; no guide can fully prepare you for that first stomach clenching appearance before the microphone or television camera. The trouble is, you don't want to risk taking part in a real media interview until you are confident you have the skills and won't make mistakes, but you won't have those skills until you've done one or more media interviews.

The answer is a *media training* course. This will give you, your employees or colleagues the chance to learn how to handle a media interview effectively in a safe learning environment where mistakes don't matter.

Several specialist companies offer such practical training in media skills. Some of these concerns are large and run courses in purpose-built radio and television studio facilities. At the other end of the spectrum is the working journalist who runs one-off courses on the client's premises. Which you choose depends on what you want to achieve and the depth of your training budget.

A typical course might involve a brief theory session to enable delegates to understand how the media works, what makes journalists 'tick' and how to handle different interview formats. The rest of the course should be taken up with practical interview training in radio, television or both.

Before you choose a trainer, establish answers to the following questions.

- Who needs the training?
- How many people do you need trained?
- What skills do they need to learn?
- How large is your training budget?

Who needs the training?
Assess your needs. Do you want the skills for yourself to help you handle a one-off awkward interview? Do you want to train a number of your staff who you expect to face the media and handle media interviews effectively? A growing number of organisations are now delegating media contact to lower management and operational tiers because they're closer to the 'coal face'. The stories they can tell will often be the ones the public want to hear or can relate to.

How many people do you need trained?
One person can lecture to hundreds, but practical interview training is best done one-to-one. The maximum size for a training group with one tutor is around six delegates. If you require a large number of people trained at one time be prepared for the media trainer to engage the services of other trainers or experienced working journalists to handle the work load effectively. If possible, spread your training load over a number of days; you may not want to take too many key personnel off-line at one time.

What skills do you need?
If you envisage having to handle only one sort of interview for, say, newspapers, then arrange a specific workshop which will focus on handling that type of media approach. On the other hand, because newspaper and broadcast interviews have much in common you may find the most cost-effective solution to a general media training requirement is to arrange a full day or more of tri-media training, encompassing press, radio and TV interviews.

Where should you hold the courses?
If you want your delegates (or yourself) trained in a real radio or
TV studio, or you want the delegates removed from the possibility of interruptions, then you'll require the training to take place
at a specialist external venue. Alternatively, if you have the
facilities to run training courses in-house it's possible to set up
very realistic simulated interview situations (such as 'down the
line' interviews) with a minimum of equipment and 'props'. This
will save you money and your staff will be closer to base if they
are required during the training course.

Cost
It's impossible to give you an accurate guide as to how much you
should expect to be charged for media training. Prices vary
enormously and depend on such factors as whether the training
facility is in a rural area or a major city, the qualifications of the
trainers and the type of training required. If you've the inclination, put the contract out to tender – you may be surprised at the
range of quotes. Don't assume the most expensive is best;
certainly you usually get what you pay for, but some smaller
consultancies, especially working journalists who train 'on the
side', may offer extremely good value for money.

Choosing a trainer
Media training isn't regulated by a professional body and the
quality of courses varies considerably. There are a few 'consult-
ants' around who believe that because they help out part-time on
a radio station at weekends they're qualified to train people in
interview technique! Others have solid journalism experience but
may have little or no training in training itself.

    Ideally what you want is a journalist with current or recent
experience in radio, TV or newspapers who also has plenty of
training experience. If yours is a specialist subject try to find a
suitably qualified trainer. If you're a scientist you can't expect a
general reporter to give you advice on interpreting complex
subjects for a general audience, so try to find a trainer with the
necessary expertise in your field. Equally, if you're in local or
national politics a tutor with experience in political journalism is
likely to give you appropriately targeted training.

    When you're talking to the media trainer you are thinking of
using ask about his or her associates. Many trainers buy in

working journalists and other relevant professionals such as camera operators to help in the practical interview sessions. Check these 'helpers' are at least proficient in their trade and preferably experienced trainers as well.

When you contact the trainer ask for their client list and contact one or two of the organisations on that list; word of mouth recommendation can pay dividends if you want to secure the services of a competent and reliable tutor.

"And finally!"

Harry and Herbert, quite independently, decided to cash in on the growing market for quality ready prepared meals. They both had the skills to make their companies work and they both did equally well at attracting the necessary finance. Soon the production lines were set up, customers had been found and both companies stood on the brink of success. That's where their paths diverged.

Herbert saw his business as making and selling meals. He certainly wasn't going to waste time talking to the media. He had a low opinion of journalists and wouldn't dream of talking to them under any circumstances.

Harry took a broader view. Right from the start he realised making meals was only part of the story. If people were to buy his meals in preference to those produced by Herbert he had to have an edge. Harry worked out that meant people had to be told about his product so he decided to risk a little of his start-up capital and commission a report from a PR company to help him set up a publicity strategy.

Having examined Harry's proposals his advisors pointed out he could capitalise on the fact that some of his products were quite unusual. In addition to the usual range of household favourites Harry had decided to run a range of meals with a historical flavour. He had been a history student and spent much of his social life at college experimenting with ancient recipes. The report recommended that Harry concentrate on publicising this side of his food business, so Harry picked a suitable name and 'Harry's Historical Fayre' was born.

The report also pointed out something Harry already half knew: his reputation would plummet if anything went wrong on the production line, or worse, someone tried to blackmail his company by spiking his product either in the factory or on the supermarket shelves. So Harry was advised to think about the unthinkable and prepare a crisis management plan – just in case. He was also advised to have media training.

So, while Herbert was putting the finishing touches to his production line, Harry took a day out to attend a media training course. He also put aside a little time to think through what he would do if it all went terribly wrong.

Ten days before the launch of his new range of meals Harry sent off a press release to all the local media. In it he made much of the fact that the product range would include ancient recipes produced to the best modern standards, and also mentioned that production line staff would be dressed in Elizabethan costume. Journalists were invited to visit his production line and sample the meals produced at a small banquet laid on specially for the launch date. They would be served by staff in costume, have access to a qualified nutritionist and be free to take samples away with them. The press release was sent off to all the local media, and, just on the off-chance, the national papers as well.

Eight days later Harry had been contacted by the both the BBC and the commercial local radio station, his local paper, the local news agency, and a national tabloid newspaper. All of them were interested in coming to interview Harry and film and photograph the production line. The local BBC radio station also asked Harry to come in and talk about his products live on that morning's breakfast show. The producer explained that this couldn't be a straightforward advertisement for Harry's business, but there was no harm in giving people tips on historical recipes – was there?

The day of the launch dawned and Harry duly turned up at the radio station and chatted about the virtues of ancient recipes. Having been media trained he knew what to expect and found the whole process remarkably painless. He put across his sales message in an entertaining and educational way and remembered to make all the points he had carefully prepared before-hand.

Later in the day, the rest of the media turned up for the actual product launch itself. The camera operators and photographers had a field day filming everything in sight, while the reporters asked every question they could think of about the differences between modern and ancient cuisine. That evening, Harry had his picture in the paper and heard and saw items on his new product line go out on the radio and television. The next day he was further gratified to find the news agency which had turned up had supplied the story to all the national papers and three had given it a brief mention. Harry was now firmly on the media map. Orders started to flood in as customers who'd seen and heard about 'Harry's Historical Fayre' asked for the new range in shops.

Meanwhile, Herbert had also had a successful product launch, but he was a little sour faced about the publicity Harry had been able to achieve. Although supermarkets had shown interest in handling his new product line, sales took a long time to take off because no one had heard of either Herbert or his meals.

Unfortunately for both Harry and Herbert things didn't go well for long. A firm which supplied both manufacturers inadvertently sold them fish which had been polluted with toxins. Members of three families were taken to hospital with food poisoning, and an investigation showed that one family had been affected by one of Herbert's products, the other two by Harry's Historical Fayre meals.

At this point the media took an interest. The two men reacted to the threat of bad publicity very differently.

Herbert issued a brief press statement through his solicitor to

Handling the media the right way gives you a free and powerful PR tool.

say his products were fine and refused to answer any questions or to take calls from the media. Unfortunately his briefing to his switchboard operator ("I won't talk to the press about our food being poisoned") was taken literally, and every media enquiry to Herbert's factory was met with: "Our company doesn't want to talk about our food being poisoned."

Harry, on the other hand, seized the opportunity to put his crisis management plan into action. He issued an immediate recall for all the products which might be affected; a hot-line was set up to take calls from concerned customers and suppliers; staff manning the hot-line were clearly briefed on what – and what not – to say; Harry then organised a press conference. At the conference he was honest about the problem, supplied exact details of the product lines affected and emphasised they'd all been recalled. He told customers how to identify the products and explained how they could be returned for a full refund. He emphasised how hygienic his production lines were, and, refusing to blame the supplier who he thought was to blame, promised a full investigation. He even ate one of his own products in front of the TV cameras to show his confidence in them. Harry was as co-operative as he could possibly be with the media and readily agreed to appear live on local radio the following morning.

Herbert meanwhile was not doing well. Under pressure from the public health authorities he had reluctantly agreed to a product recall but he was still avoiding the media. This only got the reporters' backs up and they decided to door step him as he left his factory. At first he tried to bluster his way out with a gruff "No comment", but when pressed, blamed his supplier, and then drove off.

The very different responses from both men were reported widely and the public made up its own mind as to who had their interests at heart. The crisis grumbled on for several days, and both Harry and Herbert lost money with the cost of recalling their products. But Harry's company bounced back quickly. By being open with the media, by showing concern and by keeping journalists (and therefore the public) well informed about steps being taken to resolve the problem, Harry was given the public's trust and the benefit of the doubt.

Herbert's company fared less well. The media and the public took a long time to forget his dismal performance during the crisis and as sales continued to slump Herbert was eventually forced to close his company.

Publicity can be the key to selling your product or service, it can help you put your message across to the public and offers you the means to manipulate public opinion. It's a powerful force which can lead you to riches – or rags. The key to success is knowing what you're doing. This book will have given you the knowledge you need to handle publicity the right way: to run a publicity campaign to obtain media exposure, to conduct media interviews confidently to your benefit and to handle a crisis if the publicity turns bad. The know-how you have; the skills will come with experience.

Good luck!

APPENDICES

HANDLING PRESS INTERVIEWS

Never say "No comment".	You'll sound as if you have something to hide and you may miss a valuable opportunity for positive publicity.
Be assertive.	The journalist has come to you because you know something s/he doesn't. You're important – don't be bullied. If you get a phone call out of the blue ask for time to collect your thoughts and call back, but know the deadline.
Check: who? which department? which publication?	– you're talking to. – features may pass broader comment than news. – there could be a political slant to the story.
Prepare your facts.	Have at your fingertips the who, what, when, why, how, where.
Anticipate obvious questions and pre-pare answers.	Eg Good news: What are you proposing? Why? Who will benefit? Bad news: What's gone wrong? Why? Who's responsible?

Prepare your arguments.	Turn questions to your advantage – summarise key points you want to get across and think how to work them into answers. Prepare any examples/analogies you want to use.
Brief the reporter.	Unless a specialist correspondent, the reporter will know less about the subject than you. Explain the story/context.
Give comprehensive answers.	Be unambiguous and correct any misconceptions.
Give positive answers to negative questions.	Anticipate awkward questions – think through all the *positive* things you can say. Always challenge a negative assumption.
"Off the record".	Useful for explaining the broader, confidential context to keep the story in proportion. Only use with known/trusted reporters – even then, assume all you say will be published.
Don't relax until the reporter has gone.	Some of the best quotes come from a passing shot at the door.

THE RADIO INTERVIEW

Find out all you can about the interview before-hand.	Area of questioning? Live or pre-recorded?	What sort of interview? How is material to be used?
Types of interview: In the studio. Down the line. By telephone. Pre-recorded on location.	Brief 'head-to-head'? Discussion panel? Phone-in? As above, but in unmanned studio or perhaps radio car. Most frequent in local radio. Choose a furnished room, minimise interruptions.	
Sound effects.	Be ready for recording of background sounds, if appropriate.	
Brief the reporter.	Give your name/position, context of the story and essential facts. Make clear what you are/not qualified to talk about.	

Prepare what you want to say.	Have facts at your fingertips; anticipate questions; prepare points you want to make *and make them.*
Aim for 2 or 3 points only.	Most radio interviews last only 3–4 minutes. Keep it brief. Prepare a 30–40 second summary to be used as a sound bite.
Make the most of your voice.	Speak clearly, at reasonable speed, in the appropriate mood.
Keep arguments simple.	Give clear answers – the audience only has one chance to get your meaning. Be concise so you won't be edited down.
Keep answers self-contained.	Sounds more authoritative and reduces chances of the meaning being manipulated by editing or being used out of context.
Avoid jargon.	Use everyday words/analogies to explain specialist concepts; avoid detailed discussion of procedures; use round figures.

THE TELEVISION INTERVIEW

Find out all you can about the interview before-hand.	Area of questioning? What sort of interview? Live or pre-recorded? How is material to be used?
Types of interview.	Main studio, down the line, location.
Make the most of how you look and sound.	Your image is important in television. Speak clearly/naturally. Look steadily at the interviewer or camera, as directed.
What to wear.	Be smart but comfortable. Avoid very light or very dark colours, 'busy' patterns, fussy accessories and sunglasses or Reactalite spectacles.

Prepare what you want to say.	Consider the message you want to get across and keep it to 2-3 main points. TV interviews usually only last 2-3 minutes.
Keep arguments simple.	Give clear answers – the audience only has one chance to get your meaning – and be concise so you won't be edited down. Answers of 25-40 seconds are ideal.
Keep answers self-contained.	Sounds more authoritative and reduces chance of the meaning being manipulated by editing or being used out of context.
Avoid jargon.	Use everyday words/analogies to explain specialist concepts; avoid detailed discussion of procedures; use round figures.

BROADCAST INTERVIEWS – KEY POINTS

DO	DON'T
Find out: what type of interview? whether it's live or pre-recorded? who you're up against? where, when, how interview to be used?	Say 'Good morning everyone' or refer to audience in the third person.
	Read scripted answers.
Have your facts clear.	Use jargon – you will lose the audience.
Simplify – keep to 2-3 main points.	Get complex – you will lose the audience.
Use your voice – vary pitch, tone and speed to keep the audience interested.	Waffle – if you don't know, say so.
Keep eye contact with the reporter/camera.	Get annoyed – keep cool at all times.
Correct any misconceptions.	Wear distracting clothing/accessories.
Answer the question! But turn it to your advantage.	Worry – everyone wants you to sound/look your best, it makes for better broadcasting.

CRISIS MANAGEMENT	
In advance	– anticipate likely situations – select a press spokesperson (needs good 'bedside manner') – set up efficient lines of communication
In a crisis	– give the press something to chew on as soon as you can – issue regular updates as soon as information comes in – brief staff thoroughly: *what* to say and *what not* to say
In interviews	– sound confident, concerned and authoritative – give as much information as you reasonably can – always emphasise the *positive* aspects of the situation – insist on taking questions one at a time – ask each journalist to identify him/herself – offer quotable reassurances – stress remedial action taken

WHERE TO COMPLAIN

If you feel you have been unfairly represented and a call to the journalist and perhaps one or more senior people within the particular organisation doesn't get you satisfaction, contact the following, as appropriate.

The Director
The Press Complaints Commission
1 Salisbury Square
London EC4Y 8AE   Tel: 0171 353 1248

The Secretary
The Broadcasting Complaints Commission
5 The Sanctuary
London SW1P 3JS   Tel: 0171 630 1966

The BBC Complaints Unit
BBC Broadcasting House
Portland Place
London W1A 1AA   Tel: 0171 580 4468

The Independent Television Commission
33 Foley Street
London W1P 7LB   Tel: 0171 255 3000

The Radio Authority
Holbrook House
14 Great Queen Street
London WC2B 5DG   Tel: 0171 430 2724

INDEX

RIGHT WAY
PUBLISHING POLICY

HOW WE SELECT TITLES

RIGHT WAY consider carefully every deserving manuscript. Where an author is an authority on his subject but an inexperienced writer, we provide first-class editorial help. The standards we set make sure that every **RIGHT WAY** book is practical, easy to understand, concise, informative and delightful to read. Our specialist artists are skilled at creating simple illustrations which augment the text wherever necessary.

CONSISTENT QUALITY

At every reprint our books are updated where appropriate, giving our authors the opportunity to include new information.

FAST DELIVERY

We sell **RIGHT WAY** books to the best bookshops throughout the world. It may be that your bookseller has run out of stock of a particular title. If so, he can order more from us at any time – we have a fine reputation for "same day" despatch, and we supply any order, however small (even a single copy), to any bookseller who has an account with us. We prefer you to buy from your bookseller as this reminds him of the strong underlying public demand for **RIGHT WAY** books. Readers who live in remote places, or who are housebound, or whose local bookseller is unco-operative, can order direct from us by post.

FREE

If you would like an up-to-date list of all **RIGHT WAY** titles currently available, send a stamped self-addressed envelope to

ELLIOT RIGHT WAY BOOKS,
LOWER KINGSWOOD, TADWORTH,
SURREY, KT20 6TD, U.K.